EASY
ITALIAN
COOKBOOK

EASY
ITALIAN
COOKBOOK

THE STEP-BY-STEP GUIDE TO DELICIOUSLY EASY ITALIAN FOOD AT HOME

JENNIFER DONOVAN

METRO BOOKS
NEW YORK

Copyright © Duncan Baird Publishers 2007
Text copyright © Jennifer Donovan 2007
Photography copyright © Duncan Baird Publishers 2007

This 2010 edition published by Metro Books,
by arrangement with Duncan Baird Publishers Ltd.

Managing Editor: Grace Cheetham
Editor: Cécile Landau
Managing Designer: Manisha Patel
Designer: Luana Gobbo
Studio Photography: William Lingwood
Photography Assistant: Alice Deuchar
Stylists: Bridget Sargeson and Stella Sargeson (food)
    and Helen Trent (props)

Metro Books
122 Fifth Avenue
New York, NY 10011

ISBN: 978-1-4351-2119-5

Printed and bound in Singapore

10 9 8 7 6 5 4 3 2 1

To my darling husband, who has always encouraged me to
pursue my dreams, and to my two sons, Chris and James,
who always tell it like it is.

Author's acknowledgments

My sincere thanks go to Grace Cheetham, my wonderful editor and
mentor, for sharing her enormous experience and talent and for having
faith in me. Thank you also to the skilled team at Duncan Baird, who put
my book together and turned it into something special. It has been a joy.

Publisher's note

While every care has been taken in compiling the recipes for this book,
Duncan Baird Publishers, or any other persons who have been involved
in working on this publication, cannot accept responsibility for any errors
or omissions, inadvertent or not, that may be found in the recipes or text,
nor for any problems that may arise as a result of preparing one of these
recipes. If you are pregnant or breastfeeding or have any special dietary
requirements or medical conditions, it is advisable to consult a medical
professional before following any of the recipes contained in this book.

Notes on the recipes

Unless otherwise stated:
• Use medium eggs
• Use fresh herbs
• 1 tsp = 5ml
  1 tbsp = 15ml
  1 cup = 240ml

CONTENTS

INTRODUCTION

It is hard to pinpoint the exact reason for the enduring popularity of Italian food. It could be the relaxed homey style of so many dishes; the wealth of delicious, fresh ingredients used, or the infectious delight and regional pride that Italians take in their cuisine. But none of these factors seems to account for it entirely. Italian food simply has a heart that runs deep within.

Despite modern pressures, food remains of central importance to Italian life. Sharing the table with family and friends is preserved as a ritual to this day, with its roots firmly planted in Italian values and traditions.

In the past, it was possible to divide Italy geographically according to its culinary heritage. Linked closely to its economic background, the cuisine of Italy could be loosely divided between the affluent north and the more rural south. Fresh eggs and pasta, butter, rich risotto, and creamy polenta once characterized the northern regions, while the southern parts favored olive oil, dried pastas, pizza, and tomatoes. Today, however, with increased migration around the country and the movement from rural life to city life, these culinary boundaries have blurred.

Despite this, regional boundaries remain important to the Italian people and their economy. Each region proudly produces specialty foods, including many noted cheeses and cured meats, and the provenance of each of these is strictly protected. In much the same way as France protects the provenance of its wines and other foods, Italy has developed a system known as the *denominazione d'origine protetta*, which identifies and protects the integrity and quality of a host of local products.

Italian cuisine is generally fairly simple and it is because of this simplicity that it relies heavily for its success on the best quality ingredients. Visit any town in Italy, large or small, and you will be able to find a market bursting with locally grown fruit and vegetables, where gleaming eggplants compete for attention next to dazzling red bell peppers and golden zucchini flowers, while the heady smell of fresh basil fills the air. The color, aroma, and bustle of daily living in Italy can be intoxicating.

Italian towns and cities are bursting with tiny bars, serving espresso in the morning and something stronger as the day wears on. Family-run trattorias, always friendly and welcoming, can be found dotted around the streets of most neighborhoods, and tables and chairs spill out from the numerous cafés that crowd around Italy's many piazzas. Food is something to be celebrated; something to be lingered over and shared. It is hard not to fall in love with Italy and its cuisine.

The *Easy Italian Cookbook* is designed to show you how simple it is to bring the true flavors of Italy into your own kitchen. It will take you through an understanding of some of the basic ingredients and equipment used and will guide you, step by step, through a wonderful selection of deliciously easy recipes.

You will find the recipes in the book arranged in the same order they would appear on a typical Italian table—antipasti, soup, pasta, gnocchi and risotto, meat and fish, vegetable dishes and salads, and finally desserts. You will also find a collection of menu plans to suit a wide range of specific occasions that you can follow or adapt to your own needs. Soon your family and friends will be savoring the joys of Italian food.

PART 1

THE BASICS

*A set of simple "foundation" recipes and techniques lies at the **heart** of every **great** cuisine. In this section you will find all the **basics** you will need to create wonderful Italian **meals**, ranging from recipes for simple stocks and sauces and deliciously **light** fresh pasta to several for **traditional**-style breads.*

*Keep things **simple** by making the recipes work for you. Although the stocks take time to reduce down for **optimal** flavor, they can be made well in advance. Prepare them when you have a spare moment—they can then be left to **bubble** away **happily** for hours while you carry on with something else—and keep them in the freezer for up to three months, so that they are **ready** when you need them.*

***Fresh** bread and pizza dough can be made in advance, too, then refrigerated overnight, ready to bake the next day. Many of the **sauces**—such as pesto and the basic tomato sauce for **pasta**—can be made several days ahead and kept in an airtight jar in the fridge until needed. Others, however, such as the salsa verde and béchamel, always **taste** better when they are freshly made.*

INGREDIENTS

BALSAMIC VINEGAR

Balsamic vinegar is an aged Italian vinegar from the Modena area and dates back to the 16th century. To qualify as balsamic, it must be aged for a minimum of 12 years (and can be aged for up to 150 years!), which is why the authentic product is relatively expensive. There are many inferior products on the market labeled as "balsamic" vinegar. When buying, always look for the initials MO on the label that indicates that it was made in Modena and that it has been aged correctly.

CHEESE

Fontina—A semihard cheese, it has excellent melting properties. It is made from unpasteurized cow's milk.

Gorgonzola—Made from cow's milk, this delicious blue cheese is traditionally produced in the Lombardy region. It is aged for between three to six months and varies in texture from slightly creamy to extremely creamy.

Mascarpone—Produced all over Italy, mascarpone is made from coagulated heavy cream. It is used in both savory and sweet dishes, but most commonly in desserts—it is the central ingredient in the ever-popular tiramisù ("pick-me-up" pudding, page 169).

Mozzarella—Most of what is termed mozzarella is made from cow's milk. But the finest mozzarella is produced from buffalo milk, mainly in the southern regions of Italy. Buffalo mozzarella has a higher percentage of fat and therefore has a much creamier taste. Also, the fresher the mozzarella, the creamier the texture, and it will taste better, too. Small bite-size balls of buffalo mozzarella are available, which are perfect for using in salads.

Parmesan—Parmesan, or *Parmigiano Reggiano* to give it its full Italian name, is rightly one of Italy's most famous cheeses, with recorded descriptions of it dating back as early as the 11th century. Authentic *Parmigiano Reggiano* is produced by a cooperative of around 350 cheesemakers from the provinces of Parma, Reggio Emilia, Modena, Mantua, and Bologna. Milk from other regions cannot be used.

Pecorino—Made from sheep's milk, this cheese is available in a number of different styles. One of the most widely used in cooking is the hard *Pecorino Romano* from the Lazio region of Italy around the city of Rome—hence the name.

Ricotta—This soft whey cheese is a by-product of making pecorino. Often used in cooking, it is also great with fresh fruit.

Taleggio—This semisoft, creamy cheese is made from cow's milk and has a maturation period of just 10 weeks. Usually sold as squares, it is often served with fruit as a simple and delicious ending to a meal. It can also be used in cooking.

CREAM

Although it has a milk-fat content of around 48 percent, heavy cream is used for the recipes in this book because it has the advantage of not separating when cooked. It can also be whipped.

EGGS

Unless otherwise specified, medium-size eggs should be used for all the recipes in this book.

FLOUR

The best type of flour to use for making bread is, not surprisingly, labeled "bread flour." This has a higher gluten content than all-purpose flour. Gluten is the protein found in flour that affects the texture of any baked goods made with it. Using a flour containing a high level of gluten is one of the keys to successful bread-making.

For making pasta, the best type of flour to use is very finely milled flour. It is often available as OO flour or semolina flour. This very soft flour results in a more tender, pliable pasta.

GELATIN

Although once difficult to find in supermarkets and grocery stores, leaf gelatin is now available widely. It comes in solid sheets that need to be soaked in cold water until they soften—they will then resemble a piece of wet plastic wrap. Do not soak them in hot water, as they will dissolve. Once the gelatin is wet, it will dissolve instantly when stirred into a small amount of hot liquid and can then be used as directed. Leaf gelatin is generally quicker to use than powdered gelatin (see below). Four sheets will set approximately 2½ cups of liquid.

Where required, powdered gelatin can be used instead of leaf gelatin for the recipes in this book—¼ ounce will set around 2 cups of liquid. To use, put ¼ cup of cold water in a bowl and sprinkle over ¼ ounce of powdered gelatin. Leave it to stand for five minutes, then place the bowl over a pan of gently simmering water—so that the base does not touch the water—until the gelatin mixture becomes clear. Use as directed in the recipe.

HERBS AND SPICES

Basil—This deliciously pungent herb is one of the most widely used in Italian cooking.

Bay leaf—Available dried or fresh, bay leaves are often used in stocks and soups to impart a subtle but distinctive flavor.

Black pepper—A staple in the Italian kitchen, it is at its best and most pungent when used freshly ground.

Chilies—Italian cooking most commonly uses red chilies, either fresh or dried. Bear in mind that the smaller the chili, the hotter it generally is.

Nutmeg—The seed of a plant native to Indonesia, this small nut-shaped spice can be purchased whole or ground. The best flavor comes from using the whole spice, freshly grated. It gives a warm, slightly spicy lift to recipes.

Oregano—This small, soft-leaved herb is usually added to soups and casseroles at the very last minute, giving them a wonderfully fresh flavor.

Parsley—Although available dried, fresh parsley is better by far. The flat-leaf variety is most commonly used in Italy.

Rosemary—Usually just the leaves of this herb, stripped from the stems and chopped, are used. Rosemary stems are tough, although some recipes call for whole stalks, which cook in a soup or stew and are then removed before serving.

Saffron—Derived from the crocus plant, only small quantities of this highly aromatic spice are needed. It also imparts a yellow color to dishes. The best comes from Spain.

Sage—This herb has a distinctive long, fleshy leaf and a really pungent flavor. It can be used to add a wonderful richness and depth to many recipes.

Thyme—A common addition to Italian dishes, thyme is used to flavor soups, stews, and traditional bean recipes.

LEGUMES

Legumes, such as lentils, borlotti beans, and cannellini beans, are popular in Italy. Although available canned, dried legumes can be kept indefinitely, so are a useful pantry standby. The beans are generally soaked overnight to tenderize them, then rinsed, and boiled up to an hour until they are tender.

MARSALA WINE

Made from a blend of boiled grape juice, white wine, and distilled alcohol, this sweet fortified wine was traditionally made in the west of Sicily. It is said to have been originally produced by an Englishman, John Woodhouse, in the late 18th century, as an alternative to sherry.

MUSHROOMS

Italy has more than 60 different varieties of mushrooms available and a visit to any local market in the fall will reward you with a spectacular display. Porcini are one of the most popular mushrooms in Italy, but numerous other varieties are also used. The flavor of mushrooms intensifies when they are dried and you will often see sliced porcini sold this way. In order to use them, they need to be soaked for at least 30 minutes in hot water. The soaking liquid will also impart a wonderful flavor to many dishes, such as risotto, but needs to be strained carefully before use to remove any traces of grit.

NUTS

Almonds—These are used liberally throughout Italy, especially in Sicily, where they grow in abundance.

Hazelnuts—Often used in sweet dishes, hazelnuts can be eaten raw but develop a fuller flavor when toasted. For most dishes, remove as much of the papery outer skin as possible by rubbing the toasted nuts against a strainer.

Pine nuts—Pine nuts are the small edible seeds that grow in the cone of some species of pine tree. They are a very popular addition to many Italian dishes. Although delicious when eaten raw, their flavoring is enhanced considerably by toasting. Take care, however, when doing this, as they are high in fat and will burn very easily.

Walnuts—Another popular choice of nut throughout Italy, walnuts are a central ingredient in panforte. Like most nuts, they can become bitter quite quickly—if shelled, they should ideally be stored in the fridge, where they will keep well for up to six months. They can also be frozen for up to 12 months.

OLIVES AND OLIVE OIL

Italian cooks use a wide range of green and black olives in their dishes. The color of an olive is generally of no importance, but the flavor will vary greatly, depending on the variety, the region of origin, and method that has been used for curing.

Extra-virgin olive oil is made from the first pressing of the olives and is therefore considered to be of the very best quality. It should have low acidity with a distinctive fruity aroma and flavor. Which variety you use is a matter of personal taste. Differences in flavor can be quite marked and will depend on the variety of olives used, their growing conditions and the way in which they were harvested and bottled. Heating olive oil to a high temperature generally impairs its flavor, so extra-virgin olive oil is not recommended for cooking, but is usually reserved for drizzling over food and in salad dressings.

Other types of olive oil are chemically processed after the first pressing and many of them are blended with other oils before bottling. All olive oils should be stored in a dark, airtight container, away from extremes of temperature and bright light. They should not be kept for more than two years.

PARMA HAM AND PANCETTA

Parma ham (*prosciutto di Parma*) and pancetta are just two of the cured meats for which Italy is deservedly famous. Parma ham is one of the most celebrated products of the region of Emilia-Romagna, which is renowned for its superb cuisine and wide range of gastronomic specialties. Parmesan cheese is another noted product of the region and the pigs there are fed on by-products from the making of this cheese, giving Parma ham its distinctive flavor. Parma ham is most commonly served, sliced very thinly, as part of an antipasto platter. Many other varieties of prosciutto are also available throughout Italy.

Pancetta is made from cured belly pork and is also produced all over Italy. Being relatively high in fat, it is rarely cooked and eaten on its own, but is often chopped up and added to soups and casseroles, imparting a deliciously rich flavor.

PASSATA

This is strained, crushed tomato pulp that is useful for adding to soups, pasta sauces, and other savory recipes. It can be chunky or smooth and is now widely available, ready-made in cartons and jars, from most supermarkets. It can also be made very easily at home from fresh, ripe tomatoes by simply skinning them, then pressing them through a strainer to remove the seeds.

PASTA

Two broad categories of pasta are used in Italy—fresh and dried—and, as most Italian cooks will tell you, fresh is not necessarily the best, both having their own place in the cuisine. The use of fresh homemade pasta is generally confined to the flat noodle and sheet varieties, which include pappardelle, tagliatelle, and lasagne, as well as the stuffed pastas, such as ravioli and tortellini.

Dried pasta, often made from semolina, is used for the more solid shapes, such as spaghetti, rigatoni, and penne.

Most Italian cooks today use eggs and flour to prepare homemade pasta, although in the past, in poorer parts of Italy, it was usually made with just flour and water. Because it is more porous than semolina pasta, it tends to be more absorbent and is therefore best served with creamy, buttery sauces. By comparison, dried pasta is good with oil-based and more substantial sauces—particularly the shaped pastas, as they "catch" such rich sauces well.

POLENTA

Made from coarsely ground cornmeal, polenta is an Italian staple, particularly in the northern regions. There are two varieties—the traditional slow-cooking type and the instant variety (see page 27). Although both are widely used throughout Italy, most traditional cooks would choose the slow-cooking variety for its superior flavor and texture.

RISOTTO RICE

Several different types of rice can be used to make risotto, but the three most popular varieties are Arborio, Vialone Nano, and Carnaroli. Arborio produces a "stickier" result and makes an excellent choice for really hearty risotto dishes, although it needs greater care in cooking to prevent it from becoming too stodgy. Vialone has a slightly looser consistency and gives a little more resistance to the bite. It is popular for making seafood risottos. Carnaroli, developed in the 1940s, is a relative newcomer. It is considered by many Italian cooks to be superior to all other varieties of risotto rice, since it results in dishes with a well-balanced, firm yet creamy consistency.

VEGETABLES AND FRUIT

All over Italy, markets and fruit and vegetable stores are brimming with really fresh, top quality produce, which is central to the success of so many Italian dishes. Always try to buy what is currently in season and in approximately the quantity you need at the time, because the flavor of such produce, however well kept, will deteriorate over time. Most of the fruit and vegetables used in this book, including asparagus, eggplants, zucchinis, fennel, bell peppers, tomatoes, arugula, lemons, strawberries, and peaches, are readily available, even if only for a short season every year. Cavolo nero (Tuscan kale) is one of the few exceptions and may be harder to find. This dark green, long-leafed cabbage can, however, be replaced with any other variety of cabbage, if unavailable.

YEAST

Three different types of yeast can be used for baking. The first is fresh yeast, which is often only available from a local baker or small specialist store, such as an organic wholefood outlet or a delicatessen. It comes as a compressed solid and must be stored in the fridge. The other two types are both forms of dry yeast, sold as granules in packages and readily available from the local supermarket. One, simply labeled as dry yeast, will need to be activated in warm water before use, while the other, labeled as instant yeast, can simply be stirred in with the other dry ingredients, such as flour.

Many cooks now prefer to use some form of dry yeast—especially the instant variety—since it can be stored in the pantry for a very long time, tends to be reliable, and is extremely quick and easy to use. Also, the difference between the flavor of bread that has been made with fresh yeast and that made with dry yeast is very difficult indeed to discern. All the recipes in this book involving yeast give instructions for using the instant variety, but either of the other two types may be substituted if you wish.

If you prefer to use fresh yeast, or it is the only type you have available, it is important to activate it before mixing it in with the other ingredients. This is done by warming about ½ cup of liquid (milk or water depending on the recipe) and pouring it into a mug or small bowl, then adding ½ teaspoon of sugar, stirring well, and crumbling the fresh yeast over the top. Stir gently to just combine, then leave the mixture in a warm place until it starts to foam. This should take around 10 minutes. The yeast is now ready to use.

Basic dry yeast must also be blended with a little warm water to activate it. Make sure that the liquid is not too hot—this will kill the yeast and make it inactive and you will end up with a "rock" instead of a well-risen loaf of bread. Once the yeast has begun to foam, add it to the flour mixture with the remaining ingredients, according to the recipe instructions.

Always remember that dry yeast has twice the potency of fresh yeast. For every ½ ounce of fresh yeast, you will need to use only ¼ ounce of dried yeast.

EQUIPMENT

CAST-IRON RIBBED SKILLET

This heavy pan has raised ridges across its inside base that leave an attractive pattern on food cooked in it. The food will also acquire a wonderful charbroiled flavor. These skillets can be used to cook all types of meat, fish, and vegetables quickly and easily, often without the need for any added fat, offering the bonus of a really healthy way of cooking.

CHEESE GRATER

There are a variety of designs on the market to choose from. Small microplane graters are particularly good for very hard cheeses, such as Parmesan.

COLANDER

A big colander is helpful for draining large quantities of pasta.

CUTTING BOARD

A good collection of cutting boards is essential. Make sure that they are nonporous and therefore can be cleaned well.

ELECTRIC MIXER

Both hand mixers and free-standing types are very useful in the kitchen, especially for keen bakers.

FOOD PROCESSOR

These machines are far from essential, but very convenient for quickly making pastry, pasta, and bread dough.

GARLIC PRESS

Garlic can be crushed on a board with the side of a chef's knife (sprinkle the garlic with salt to help with the crushing action), but many cooks find it quicker to use a garlic press.

ICE CREAM MAKER

If you truly love gelato, then this can be a good investment. A wide variety is available, from battery-operated models to large machines with their own built-in freezer.

IMMERSION HAND BLENDER

Sometimes known as a "wand," this type of electric blender can process food without having to remove it from the pan it has been cooked in. It is great for puréeing soups and sauces.

JUICE EXTRACTOR

These range from simple hand-operated citrus presses to large electrical appliances that can extract the juice from any type of fruit or vegetable.

KNIVES

The cook's most important tool, when preparing any type of cuisine, is a set of sharp, good quality knives. This should include an 8 inch all-purpose chef's knife, one or two small paring knives, and a serrated-edged knife. Other knives, such as a carving or boning knife, can be added to the basic kit as required. For preparing herbs, Italian cooks often prefer to use a *mezzaluna*, which consists of a curved-blade knife with a handle at each end that is used in a rocking motion to chop herbs really finely.

PASTA MACHINE

Many Italians still roll out pasta by hand, but a pasta machine makes the job much easier. It is best to buy the type that clamps onto a worktop and pushes the pasta out through a set of rollers that is rotated by hand. Electric machines that also mix the pasta dough tend to give a poorer result.

POTATO RICER

Cooked potatoes are pressed through this device, resembling a large garlic press, to create a soft purée—great for gnocchi.

SAUCEPANS

You will need a full range of saucepans, from the very small (for melting butter or heating milk) to the very large (for boiling water for pasta or for preparing stocks and stews). Remember that pans with a thick, heavy base will conduct heat better, and so cook more quickly and evenly than cheaper, more lightweight pans.

SAUTÉ PAN

This is an invaluable tool in any kitchen. A sauté pan differs from a skillet in that it has slightly higher, sloping edges, making it perfect for panfrying meats and making sauces. The pan's wide surface will allow excess liquid to evaporate easily if needed and the sloping edges will allow the steam to escape rather than staying in the pan and steaming the food. A handy size for a sauté pan is about 10 inches in diameter.

SLOTTED SPOON

This simple utensil will prove endlessly useful for lifting cooked food out of hot water or fat without having to drain the entire pan.

SPRINGFORM CAKE PANS

The springform design of the cake pan makes removing the contents much easier. They are available in a variety of sizes.

TONGS

Tongs make turning over food, such as a piece of meat or fish, halfway through cooking, really quick and easy.

VEGETABLE PEELER

This is useful, not only for removing the skin from potatoes and carrots, but also for slicing them up really thinly. The long type with a pointed tip can also be used to core apples.

WOODEN SPOONS

Cheap and hard-wearing, a set of these is always handy, since they can be used for stirring or mixing any food, hot or cold.

STOCKS AND SAUCES

BEEF STOCK
BRODO DI MANZO

MAKES 2 QUARTS
PREPARATION TIME: 35 MINUTES   COOKING TIME: 4 HOURS

2¼ pounds **beef** bones

1 **onion** (skin left on), roughly chopped

1 **carrot**, roughly chopped

1 stalk **celery**, roughly chopped

4 **black peppercorns**

1 **bay leaf**

1 sprig **thyme**

1 small handful **flat-leaf parsley**, roughly chopped

1 gallon cold **water**

1 **HEAT** the oven to 400°F. Place the beef bones on a baking sheet and roast in the hot oven around 30 minutes, or until well browned all over.

2 **REMOVE** any fat from the bones, then transfer them to a large saucepan. Add all of the remaining ingredients.

3 **BRING** to a boil. Skim off any froth and sediment from the surface, then lower the heat, and leave to simmer very gently for 4 hours, skimming often. Remove from the heat and leave to cool, then strain.

4 **REFRIGERATE** overnight, then remove any fat that has collected on the surface. Use as required. It will keep for 3 to 4 days in the fridge and up to 3 months in the freezer.

CHICKEN STOCK
BRODO DI POLLO

MAKES 2 QUARTS
PREPARATION TIME: 15 MINUTES   COOKING TIME: 2½ HOURS

If you have trouble finding chicken carcasses, replace with chicken wings. They will render more fat, but this can easily be removed from the surface of the stock after it has been chilled overnight in the fridge.

2¼ pounds fresh **chicken** carcasses, chopped

1 **onion** (skin left on), cut into quarters

1 **carrot**, roughly chopped

1 bulb **garlic**, cut in half horizontally

1 stalk **celery**, roughly chopped

4 **black peppercorns**

1 small handful **flat-leaf parsley**, roughly chopped

2 **bay leaves**

1½ gallons cold **water**

1 **PLACE** all of the ingredients in a large saucepan and bring gently to a boil.

2 **SKIM** off any foam and sediment from the surface, then lower the heat and leave to simmer around 2½ hours.

3 **STRAIN** the stock through a fine strainer into a clean bowl. Cover and leave to cool completely.

4 **REFRIGERATE** overnight, then skim off any fat from the surface and use as required. It will keep for 3 to 4 days in the fridge and up to 3 months in the freezer.

FISH STOCK
BRODO DI PESCE

MAKES 2 QUARTS
PREPARATION TIME: 10 MINUTES   COOKING TIME: 20 MINUTES

¼ stick **butter**

1 **onion**, roughly chopped

4 ounces **fish** bones, washed and chopped

½ cup **dry white wine**

2½ quarts cold **water**

1 **bay leaf**

4 **black peppercorns**

1 small handful **flat-leaf parsley**, roughly chopped

1 small stalk **celery**, roughly chopped

1 **MELT** the butter in a large saucepan over a low heat. Add the onion and cook 2 to 3 minutes until soft but not brown. Add the fish bones and cook about 1 minute, then pour over the white wine, turn up the heat, and boil until all the wine has evaporated.

2 **ADD** the water, bay leaf, peppercorns, parsley, and celery and bring to a boil. Skim off any froth and sediment from the surface, then turn down the heat, and leave to simmer gently 20 minutes, skimming often.

3 **STRAIN** and leave to cool. Use as needed. It will keep 3 to 4 days in the fridge and up to 3 months in the freezer.

VEGETABLE STOCK
BRODO DI VERDURA

MAKES 2 PINTS
PREPARATION TIME: 15 MINUTES   COOKING TIME: 1 HOUR

1 stalk **celery**, roughly chopped, plus any leaves from the top of the stalk

1 **carrot**, roughly chopped

1 **onion**, skin removed and sliced

1 bulb **garlic**, cut in half horizontally

2 **bay leaves**

6 **black peppercorns**

1 small handful **flat-leaf parsley**, roughly chopped

3½ pints cold **water**

1 **PLACE** all of the ingredients in a large saucepan and bring to a boil over a medium heat.

2 **LOWER** the heat and leave to simmer gently 1 hour. Remove from the heat and leave to cool.

3 **STRAIN** the stock, pushing down on the vegetables gently to extract the maximum amount of flavor. Use as required. It will keep up to 4 days in the fridge and up to 3 months in the freezer.

BÉCHAMEL SAUCE

MAKES **2** PINTS
PREPARATION TIME: **10** MINUTES   COOKING TIME: **10** MINUTES

This simple white sauce makes its appearance in the lasagne recipe on page 85, but is also added to all kinds of other dishes.

2 pints **milk**

½ small **onion**

1 **bay leaf**

1 whole **clove**

6 tablespoons **butter**

⅔ cup **all-purpose flour**

salt and freshly ground **black pepper**

grating of fresh **nutmeg**

1 **PLACE** the milk, onion, bay leaf, and clove in a medium saucepan and heat gently. As soon as the milk starts to simmer, remove from the heat, and leave on one side for at least 10 minutes. Strain, discarding the solids, and set aside.

2 **MELT** the butter in a clean saucepan. Stir in the flour, then cook over a low heat for 2 to 3 minutes, taking care not to let the mixture brown. Remove from the heat.

3 **WHISK** the milk into the butter and flour mixture, then return to a low heat and continue to whisk until the sauce is smooth and thick. Leave to simmer very gently about 3 minutes. Season to taste with salt, pepper, and nutmeg and use as required.

BLACK OLIVE TAPENADE
PASTA D'OLIVE

MAKES **1** CUP
PREPARATION TIME: **15** MINUTES

7 ounces good quality **black olives**, pitted

4 ounces canned **anchovy** fillets, rinsed

2 heaped teaspoons **capers**, drained and rinsed

2 cloves **garlic**, peeled

grated zest and juice of 1 **lemon**

⅔ cup **extra-virgin olive oil**

1 **PLACE** all of the ingredients in a blender or food processor and process until smooth.

2 **STORE** in the refrigerator up to 1 month and use as required—as a flavoring or as a savory dip with chunks of crusty fresh bread.

FRESH TOMATO SAUCE
SALSA FRESCA DI POMODORO

MAKES 2 CUPS
PREPARATION TIME: 15 MINUTES   COOKING TIME: 30 MINUTES

Try to use ripe, in-season tomatoes for this recipe. Canned tomatoes, however, can be substituted when good fresh ones are unavailable.

2 tablespoons olive oil

1 onion, diced

1 clove garlic, crushed

2 pounds fresh plum tomatoes, peeled, deseeded, and chopped

6 fresh basil leaves

1 teaspoon balsamic vinegar

1 teaspoon sugar

salt and freshly ground black pepper

1 HEAT the oil in a wide-based skillet. Add the onion and cook for 3 to 4 minutes until it is soft and transparent. Add the garlic and cook for another minute.

2 STIR in the tomatoes, basil, balsamic vinegar, and sugar and leave to simmer 30 minutes, stirring occasionally.

3 SEASON to taste with salt and pepper, then tip into a blender or food processor and process until smooth. Use as required. It can be stored in the fridge 2 to 3 days, but is best stored frozen—use within 3 months.

VARIATIONS

TOMATO AND ROASTED RED BELL PEPPER SAUCE— Cut 2 red bell peppers in half lengthwise, remove and discard the seeds, and arrange, skin side up, on a lightly oiled baking sheet. Place under a hot broiler for 5 to 10 minutes until the skin is really black and burnt and the flesh is just starting to soften. Remove from the broiler, cover loosely with a clean cloth, and put to one side until cold, then peel off the charred skin. Roughly chop the softened flesh and add to the sauce mixture along with the seasoning at the beginning of Step 3 of the basic recipe.

TOMATO, ANCHOVY, AND OLIVE SAUCE—As soon as the onions are soft and transparent (in Step 1 of the basic recipe) add 6 anchovy fillets, which have been drained and rinsed, to the skillet. Cook over a low heat until the anchovies start to break up, then toss in the garlic, and continue as for the basic recipe, substituting a large handful of roughly chopped flat-leaf parsley for the basil. Rinse, pit, and chop a handful of green olives and stir into the smooth sauce after it has been processed in the blender or food processor.

BASIC TOMATO SAUCE FOR PIZZA
SALSA DI POMODORO PER PIZZA

MAKES **1** CUP
PREPARATION TIME: **5** MINUTES   COOKING TIME: **15** TO **20** MINUTES

This makes a thick, rich tomato sauce that is just perfect for pizza.

3 cups canned **tomatoes**, chopped
1 tablespoon **olive oil**
1 teaspoon dried **basil**
1 teaspoon dried **oregano**
1 clove **garlic**, crushed
2 tablespoons **tomato paste**
salt and freshly ground **black pepper**

1 PLACE all the ingredients in a medium-sized saucepan, seasoning to taste with salt and pepper. Bring to a boil.
2 LOWER the heat and leave to simmer 15 to 20 minutes, or until the sauce has thickened, stirring occasionally. Set aside to cool slightly, then transfer to a blender or food processor, and process until smooth.
3 ALLOW the sauce to cool completely, then use as required. It can be stored in the fridge up to 1 week and in the freezer up to 3 months.

BASIL PESTO
PESTO

MAKES **1** CUP
PREPARATION TIME: **15** MINUTES

This simple sauce is absolutely bursting with flavor. It can be made in advance and kept in the fridge, ready to simply stir into a plate of freshly cooked pasta to create a quick and delicious meal. To store, place in an airtight container, top with a splash of extra-virgin olive oil, and refrigerate. It will keep for approximately 2 weeks.

3 large handfuls fresh **basil leaves**
1 ounce **pine nuts**
2 large cloves **garlic**, chopped
1 tablespoon **sea** (or **kosher**) **salt**
freshly ground **black pepper**
⅔ cup **extra-virgin olive oil**
¼ cup grated **Parmesan cheese**

1 PLACE the basil, pine nuts, and garlic in a large bowl. Add salt and pepper to taste.
2 ADD the olive oil and blend, using a hand mixer or blender, to form a paste. Alternatively, process the ingredients in a blender or food processor.
3 STIR in the Parmesan cheese, taste, and readjust the seasoning if necessary. Use as required.

BASIC RECIPES

FRESH PASTA

SERVES **4** AS A MAIN COURSE; **8** AS AN APPETIZER
PREPARATION TIME: **30** MINUTES
COOKING TIME: **4** MINUTES, PLUS **30** MINUTES RESTING TIME

The silky texture of freshly made pasta is well worth the effort that goes into preparing it yourself at home. For the best result, use specialized 00 flour—often labeled as "pasta flour"—which is now readily available from many supermarkets as well as specialty stores. A food processor makes mixing the dough easier, but it can also be mixed by hand. To roll out the pasta, you ideally need a good quality manual pasta machine.

2 cups 00 (pasta) **flour**

6 large **egg yolks**

1 **egg**

1½ tablespoons **olive oil**

1 tablespoon **milk**

1 **PLACE** the flour in the bowl of a food processor. Whisk together the egg yolks, egg, oil, and milk in a separate bowl.

2 **WITH** the motor running, slowly pour the liquid mixture through the feeding tube onto the flour in the processor until a soft ball of dough is just starting to form. Take care not to add too much liquid. Depending on the weather, the dough may need more or less to come together. Put in plastic wrap, set aside, and allow to rest for 30 minutes.

3 **DIVIDE** the dough in two and set one half aside in a cool place in plastic wrap to prevent it from drying out.

4 **SET** the pasta machine to its widest setting and use to roll out the unwrapped half of dough. Fold the rolled dough in

half and roll it once more through the machine. Repeat this process 10 more times, folding the dough in half each time before passing it through the machine.

5 **CONTINUE** rolling the dough in this way, but without folding it in half, and lower the setting on the machine by one notch each time, until it has passed through on the second narrowest setting (any narrower and it tends to fall apart).

6 **LAY** the sheet of dough on a lightly floured board. Cut into shapes with a sharp knife or cutter and leave to dry.

7 **REPEAT** with the remaining half of the dough.

8 **BRING** a large pot of salted water to a boil. Add the pasta and stir well to prevent it sticking. Return to a boil, lower the heat, and leave to simmer about 4 minutes, or until the pasta has floated to the top and is paler in color. Drain and serve immediately with your chosen sauce.

VARIATIONS

PASTA WITH FRESH HERBS—Add 3 tablespoons of finely chopped, fresh, mixed herbs, such as oregano, flat-leaf parsley, and thyme to the flour. Proceed as for basic recipe.

TOMATO PASTA—Beat 2 tablespoons of tomato paste into the egg mixture. Proceed as for the basic recipe.

SPINACH PASTA—Use only 3 egg yolks. Add 2 ounces cooked spinach, that has been squeezed until very dry, to flour in the food processor and pulse briefly to combine. Proceed as for the basic recipe.

"WET" POLENTA

SERVES **4**   PREPARATION TIME: **10** MINUTES   COOKING TIME: **1** HOUR

With casseroles and similar dishes, polenta is usually served "wet" (sometimes described as "soft"). This means that it has simply been cooked in water or stock and served straight from the pot, so that it resembles mashed potato.

Traditional slow-cook polenta will take around 1 hour to prepare, simmering gently on the stove. You can vary the flavor by adding fresh herbs or freshly grated Parmesan cheese to it before serving.

An instant variety of polenta is also available which takes very little time to prepare, although most Italians would argue that the flavor is very poor. However, for the time-starved cook it makes a good substitute.

5½ cups **chicken stock** or **water**

1 cup **polenta** (not instant)

2 tablespoons **butter**, cut into pieces

salt and freshly ground **black pepper**

1 **BRING** the water or stock to a boil in a large saucepan. Remove from the heat and whisk in the polenta in a steady stream. Lower the heat to a simmer and return to the stove.

2 **SIMMER** very gently 50 to 60 minutes, stirring from time to time, until thick and creamy. Stir in the butter, then season to taste with salt and pepper. Keep warm until required.

"DRY" POLENTA

SERVES **4**   PREPARATION TIME: **13** MINUTES
COOKING TIME: **1** HOUR **5** MINUTES, PLUS COOLING TIME

Crisp, freshly fried pieces of "dry" polenta are also very popular, served as an accompaniment to broiled meat or fish, or as a base for antipasti.

ingredients as for **"wet" polenta**
olive oil

1 **PREPARE** the "wet" polenta according to the instruction, left.

2 **POUR** the the cooked "wet" polenta into a large, lightly greased baking sheet and spread out to form a layer about 1½ inches thick. Put to one side and leave to cool completely.

3 **CUT** the cooled polenta into wedges or squares and drizzle each with a little olive oil.

4 **HEAT** a ribbed or any heavy-based skillet until hot. Place the pieces of polenta in the skillet and charbroil about 2 to 3 minutes on each side until lightly golden. Alternatively, the polenta may be cooked under a hot broiler. Use as required.

BASIC PIZZA DOUGH
PASTA BASE PER PIZZA

MAKES 2 x 12 INCH PIZZA BASES OR APPROXIMATELY
36 INDIVIDUAL PIZZAS
PREPARATION TIME: 25 MINUTES, PLUS 1 HOUR PROVING TIME

4 cups **bread flour**, plus extra
    for kneading

1 tablespoon **salt**

1 teaspoon **sugar**

2 teaspoons **instant yeast** *(see page 15)*

freshly ground **black pepper**

2 tablespoons **olive oil**, plus extra for oiling

1½ cups warm **water**

1 MIX together the flour, salt, sugar, yeast, and pepper
to taste in a large bowl and make a well in the center.

2 POUR the olive oil into the well, then mix in with
just enough warm water to form a soft dough.

3 REMOVE the dough from the bowl and place on a
lightly floured surface. Knead around 10 minutes until
the dough is smooth and elastic, adding extra flour to
the surface as required.

4 PLACE the dough in a lightly oiled bowl, cover with
plastic wrap, and leave to prove in a warm place about
1 hour until doubled in size.

PIZZA

MAKES 2 x 12 INCH PIZZAS
PREPARATION TIME: 10 MINUTES COOKING TIME: 10 TO 15 MINUTES

1 recipe quantity **basic pizza dough** *(see left)*

1 recipe quantity **basic tomato sauce for
  pizza** *(see page 24)*

topping *(see below)*

1 HEAT the oven to 425°F. Knead the risen pizza dough on a
lightly floured surface 2 to 3 minutes.

2 DIVIDE the dough in half and roll out each half to fit into
a lightly greased pizza pan 12 inches in diameter.

3 SPOON over some of the tomato sauce, then add your
chosen topping. Bake in the heated oven about 10 to 15
minutes until the topping is melted and golden. Serve.

TOPPING SUGGESTIONS

PIZZA MARGHERITA—Scatter 6 ounces grated mozzarella
cheese and 8 roughly torn fresh basil leaves over the tomato
sauce on the pizza base.

PIZZA AI FUNGHI—Sauté ¾ pound sliced mushrooms in a
little olive oil until soft. Spoon over the tomato sauce on the
pizza base, then sprinkle over 2 ounces grated mozzarella.

PIZZA MARINARA—Scatter 3 chopped garlic cloves and a
handful of chopped fresh oregano over the tomato sauce on
the pizza base. Arrange 6 anchovy fillets with 8 roughly torn
fresh basil leaves on top, then drizzle over a little olive oil.

FOCACCIA

SERVES 4 TO 6
PREPARATION TIME: 20 MINUTES
COOKING TIME: 20 MINUTES, PLUS 1 HOUR PROVING TIME

4 cups **bread flour**, plus extra for kneading

2 teaspoons **sea** (or **kosher**) **salt**, plus 1 tablespoon for sprinkling

½ teaspoon **sugar**

2 teaspoons **instant yeast** *(see page 15)*

2 tablespoons **olive oil**, plus extra for drizzling

about 3 cups warm **water**

1 **HEAT** the oven to 450°F.

2 **MIX** the flour, 2 teaspoons sea salt, sugar, and yeast together in a large bowl and make a well in the center.

3 **POUR** the olive oil into the well and mix into the flour mixture with enough warm water to form a soft dough.

4 **TIP** the dough onto a lightly floured surface and knead about 10 minutes, or until it springs back when pressed gently. Add extra flour to the work surface as required.

5 **PLACE** the dough in a clean bowl, cover with plastic wrap, and leave in a warm place 1 hour, until doubled in size.

6 **REMOVE** the dough from the bowl, place on a lightly floured surface, and knead again for 2 to 3 minutes until smooth. Place on a large baking sheet and gently pull and stretch the dough to cover the tray. Drizzle over a little olive oil and sprinkle with the remaining tablespoon of sea salt. Leave in a warm place 30 minutes to rise. Once the dough has risen, make several rows of indentations across the surface.

7 **BAKE** in the heated oven 20 to 25 minutes until golden brown and slightly risen. Test to see if fully cooked by tapping the base—it should sound hollow.

8 **DRIZZLE** a little more olive oil over the top and leave to cool on a wire rack about 15 minutes. Serve, cut into slices.

VARIATIONS

FOCACCIA AL ROSMARINO—Mix 1 tablespoon of dried rosemary and 1 tablespoon of finely chopped, fresh rosemary, into the flour, salt, sugar, and yeast mixture before mixing in the olive oil and warm water to form the dough. Also, place small sprigs of fresh rosemary in the indentations made across the surface of the dough (see Step 6, above) just before it goes into the oven.

FOCACCIA WITH SUN-DRIED TOMATOES—Mix 3 tablespoons of finely chopped sun-dried tomatoes into the flour, salt, sugar, and yeast mixture before mixing in the olive oil and warm water to form the dough. Also, place small pieces of sun-dried tomatoes in the indentations across the surface of the dough (see Step 6, above) just before it goes into the oven.

EVERYDAY WHITE LOAF

PANE BIANCO

MAKES **1** LARGE LOAF
PREPARATION TIME: **30** MINUTES
COOKING TIME: **40** TO **50** MINUTES, PLUS **1** HOUR PROVING TIME

The smell of freshly baked bread is absolutely irresistible.

5½ cups **bread flour**, plus extra for kneading

2 teaspoons **instant yeast** *(see page 15)*

1 teaspoon **sugar**

1 tablespoon **salt**

1 cup warm **water**

1 cup warm **milk**

2 tablespoons **extra-virgin olive oil**

olive oil, plus extra for greasing

1 **egg**, lightly beaten

2 tablespoons **sesame seeds**

1 COMBINE the flour, yeast, sugar, and salt in a large bowl. Make a well in the center and set aside.

2 MIX together the warm water, warm milk, and olive oil in a small bowl. Pour about three-quarters of the liquid into the well in the flour mixture and gradually mix in to form a soft dough. Use more of the remaining liquid if necessary.

3 PLACE the dough on a lightly floured surface and knead well about 10 minutes until it springs back easily when pressed gently.

4 TRANSFER the dough to a clean, lightly oiled, large bowl. Cover with plastic wrap and leave in a warm place about 1 hour, or until the dough has doubled in size.

5 HEAT the oven to 400°F. Place the dough on a lightly floured surface and flatten and shape it to form a large, 1 inch thick circle. Brush with a little of the lightly beaten egg and roll up, tucking in the sides, to form a neat package.

6 GREASE a baking sheet with a little more olive oil and place the shaped dough on top. Brush with the remaining beaten egg and sprinkle over the sesame seeds. Slash the top with a sharp knife in two or three places. Put to the side in a warm place a further 30 minutes until well risen.

7 SPRINKLE over a little cold water, then bake in the heated oven 40 to 50 minutes until golden brown and well risen. To test if fully cooked, tap the base of the loaf—it should sound hollow. Leave to cool on a wire cooling rack at least 30 minutes before serving.

LITTLE BREADSTICKS

GRISSINI

MAKES **30** GRISSINI
PREPARATION TIME: **20** MINUTES
COOKING TIME: **18** TO **20** MINUTES, PLUS **1** HOUR PROVING TIME

These delicious little breadsticks make a wonderful addition to a platter of antipasto. Their flavor can be varied by mixing in a small handful of finely chopped fresh herbs, such as oregano, thyme, or rosemary, when preparing the dough. They can also be flavored by sprinkling some sesame or poppy seeds, along with the crushed sea salt, over the top of the rolled-out "sausages" of dough, just before baking.

3 cups **bread flour**, plus extra for kneading

2 teaspoons **instant yeast** *(see page 15)*

1 tablespoon **salt**

1 cup warm **water**

3 tablespoons **olive oil**

2 tablespoons **sea** (or **kosher**) **salt**, lightly crushed

1 **PLACE** the flour, yeast, and salt into a large bowl and combine together thoroughly. Make a well in the center and set on one side.

2 **MIX** together the warm water and 1 tablespoon of the olive oil in a small bowl and pour half of this into the well in the center of the flour mixture. Gradually stir in and bring together to make a soft dough, adding more of the remaining liquid if required. The dough should be slightly sticky but not wet. Turn out onto a lightly floured surface.

3 **KNEAD** for about 10 minutes, until smooth and elastic. The dough should spring back when pressed gently. Transfer to a clean, lightly oiled bowl and cover with plastic wrap. Leave in a warm place about 1 hour until the dough has doubled in size.

4 **HEAT** the oven to 400°F.

5 **REMOVE** the risen dough from the bowl and transfer to a lightly floured surface. Knead well about 2 to 3 minutes until the dough is smooth and silky. Divide into 30 pieces, then roll each piece into a long "sausage" shape about 8 inches long. Arrange these on baking sheets that have been lined with parchment paper.

6 **BRUSH** lightly with the remaining olive oil, then sprinkle over the crushed sea salt. Bake in the heated oven 18 to 20 minutes until the breadsticks are golden brown. Allow to cool a little, then serve warm.

PART 2

THE RECIPES

A traditional Italian meal has many components, from the **delicious** little antipasti **morsels**, often found in bars around the country and served with drinks at home, to simple **homemade** desserts. A meal would be incomplete without a pasta or risotto course, which is usually served as the first course or **primo piatto**, followed by a meat or fish course with some **simple** vegetables and salads.

In this chapter you will find a selection of **easy** recipes that characterize the **flavors** of the different Italian regions. Many may be familiar to you from your own **travels** and all of them can be easily reproduced in your own home.

The key to the success of all the recipes in this section is in the **quality** of the ingredients—for the best results it is always vital to use the **freshest** ingredients you can find. The **good** news is that all of the produce needed to prepare the recipes in this book is now widely **available**. But if you do have trouble sourcing an **ingredient** or finding the very best quality, do not worry about using a good substitute. The recipe may well be the **better** for it.

CHARBROILED VEGETABLE SALAD

INSALATA DI VERDURE GRIGLIATE

SERVES 4   PREPARATION TIME: 15 MINUTES   COOKING TIME: 20 MINUTES

The vibrant colors and flavors of this salad make it perfect for any weather.

½ pound fresh **asparagus**

3 **zucchinis**

3 **bell peppers** (in a variety of colors)

1 large **eggplant**

3 tablespoons **olive oil**

3 cloves **garlic**, crushed

salt and freshly ground **black pepper**

¼ pound **cherry tomatoes**

5 tablespoons **extra-virgin olive oil**

2 tablespoons **balsamic vinegar** (see page 10)

1 large handful **basil leaves**, roughly torn

1 **TRIM** off and discard any woody parts from the ends of the asparagus stems, then plunge them into a pan of boiling salted water 2 minutes. Drain and rinse under cold running water to stop further cooking. Leave to dry on paper towels.

2 **CUT** the zucchinis diagonally into ⅓ inch thick slices. Trim the bell peppers and cut into quarters, discarding the seeds and membrane. Slice the eggplant horizontally. Place all the prepared vegetables in a large bowl with the asparagus. Add the olive oil, 2 of the garlic cloves, and salt and pepper to taste. Toss to coat the vegetables well.

3 **HEAT** a large ribbed skillet (see page 16) until hot and use to cook the vegetables until lightly browned and just soft. You may need to do this in batches, keeping cooked vegetables warm while preparing the remainder. Arrange on a large serving platter and top with the cherry tomatoes.

4 **WHISK** together the extra-virgin olive oil, balsamic vinegar, and remaining garlic in a small bowl. Season to taste with salt and pepper, then pour it over the vegetables, and toss lightly. Scatter the basil leaves over the salad. Serve warm or at room temperature.

BAKED MUSSELS WITH CRISPY HERB BREADCRUMBS

COZZE GRATINATE

SERVES 4   PREPARATION TIME: 30 MINUTES   COOKING TIME: 5 MINUTES

The crunchiness of the topping in this dish works beautifully with the creamy softness of the mussels.

---

1 pound fresh **mussels**

½ cup dry **white wine**

1 clove **garlic**, chopped

3 tablespoons **olive oil**

3 cups fresh **white breadcrumbs**

1 large handful **flat-leaf parsley**, chopped

juice of 1 **lemon**, reserving ⅛ lemon wedge to serve

2 tablespoons **extra-virgin olive oil**

freshly ground **black pepper**

1 **CLEAN** the mussels thoroughly by soaking in plenty of cold water. Use a sharp knife to remove any barnacles and the fibrous "beard" from the side of the mussels. Discard any with broken shells.

2 **PLACE** the mussels in a large saucepan and add the wine and garlic. Cover and cook over a high heat 3 to 4 minutes. Strain off the liquid, discard any mussels that have not opened, and leave to cool. Remove the mussels from their shells and set them on one side, along with half of the empty shells.

3 **HEAT** the olive oil in a large sauté pan (see page 17) and add the breadcrumbs. Stir well until lightly browned and then add the parsley.

4 **HEAT** the oven to 425°F. Place each mussel in a half shell and top with some of the breadcrumb mixture. Arrange in a single layer in a shallow baking dish, drizzle over the lemon juice and extra-virgin olive oil, then bake in the hot oven 5 minutes until the breadcrumbs are golden. Season to taste with pepper and serve, accompanied by lemon wedge.

EGGPLANT WITH TOMATO SAUCE AND CHEESE

MELANZANE ALLA PARMIGIANA

**SERVES 4 TO 6 PREPARATION TIME: 25 MINUTES
COOKING TIME: 20 MINUTES**

Bursting with the fragrance of fresh tomatoes and basil, this makes a great appetizer as well as a good light lunch, served with a simple green salad.

4 large **eggplants**

5 tablespoons **olive oil**

freshly ground **black pepper**

1 handful fresh **basil**, shredded

½ pound grated **mozzarella cheese**

1 recipe quantity **fresh tomato sauce**
  (see page 23)

4 tablespoons freshly grated **Parmesan cheese**

1 **HEAT** the oven to 400°F. Slice the eggplants into circles, approximately ¼ inch thick. Brush both sides lightly with the olive oil and and arrange in a single layer on a large baking sheet. Season well with pepper.

2 **BAKE** in the hot oven about 15 minutes, or until the eggplants are beginning to soften.

3 **LAYER** the baked eggplants in a lightly greased, ovenproof dish with the basil, mozzarella cheese, and tomato sauce.

4 **SPRINKLE** over the Parmesan cheese and grind over black pepper to taste. Bake in the hot oven 15 to 20 minutes until golden brown and bubbling. Leave to cool slightly before serving.

CROSTINI WITH GARLIC, TOMATO, AND ANCHOVY

CROSTINI CON AGLIO, POMODORO E ACCIUGA

MAKES 24   PREPARATION TIME: 15 MINUTES   COOKING TIME: 10 MINUTES

These crispy little crostini make the perfect partner to predinner drinks. They can be served with different toppings (see page 42).

2 day-old **breadsticks** *(see page 31)*

2 tablespoons **olive oil**

salt and freshly ground **black pepper**

TOPPING:

1 small clove **garlic**, crushed

2 medium **tomatoes**, peeled, deseeded, and diced

1 **avocado**, diced

6 **anchovy** fillets (in salt), rinsed and diced

1 teaspoon **lemon juice**

1 tablespoon **extra-virgin olive oil**

6 fresh **basil leaves**, roughly chopped

freshly ground **black pepper**

1 **HEAT** the oven to 350°F. Cut each breadstick into 12 slices and arrange in a single layer on a baking sheet. Drizzle with the olive oil and season well with salt and pepper.

2 **BAKE** in the hot oven about 10 minutes until lightly browned. Remove the crostini from the oven and leave to cool slightly. (If not using immediately, they may be stored in an airtight tin and warmed briefly in the oven before topping and serving.)

3 **PREPARE** the topping by mixing together the garlic, tomatoes, avocado, and anchovies in a bowl, then stir in the lemon juice, extra-virgin olive oil, and basil leaves. Season to taste with black pepper.

4 **PLACE** a heaped teaspoon of the topping mixture on each of the warm crostini. Serve immediately.

CROSTINI WITH GORGONZOLA AND BLACK OLIVE TAPENADE

CROSTINI CON GORGONZOLA E PASTA D'OLIVE

MAKES 24   PREPARATION TIME: 15 MINUTES

The creaminess of the Gorgonzola contrasts wonderfully with the saltiness of the tapenade.

---

1 recipe quantity **crostini** *(see page 41)*

1 small clove **garlic**, cut in half

1 tablespoon **extra-virgin olive oil**

6 ounces **Gorgonzola cheese**

4 tablespoons **black olive tapenade** *(see page 20)*

1 **WARM** the crostini slightly in a hot oven, if not freshly baked. Then rub each one well with the cut surface of the garlic clove and drizzle over a little of the extra-virgin olive oil.

2 **SPREAD** 1 teaspoon of the Gorgonzola cheese over the top of each of the crostini, using a knife. Arrange on a serving platter.

3 **TOP** each of the crostini with a little of the black olive tapenade and serve immediately.

TUNA CARPACCIO
CARPACCIO DI TONNO

SERVES **4** PREPARATION TIME: **10** MINUTES, PLUS **1** HOUR FREEZING TIME

The tuna for this recipe must be of the highest quality and really fresh. Ask at the fish counter for the tail end of the tuna, as this is easier to slice. The softness of the tuna combined with the dressing is absolutely sublime.

10 ounce piece fresh, top quality ("sashimi grade") **tuna**

juice and grated zest of 2 **lemons**

½ cup **extra-virgin olive oil**

1 clove **garlic**, crushed

2 tablespoons **flat-leaf parsley**, finely chopped

salt and freshly ground **black pepper**

1 large handful **arugula**

2 tablespoons **Parmesan cheese** shavings

1 **PLACE** the tuna in the freezer on a medium setting about 1 hour until it is firm but not hard.

2 **MAKE** a dressing by whisking together the lemon juice and zest, olive oil, garlic, and parsley in a small bowl until well combined. Season to taste with salt and pepper.

3 **REMOVE** the tuna from the freezer and cut into very thin slices. Divide these equally among 4 serving plates. Drizzle a tablespoon of the dressing over each serving.

4 **TOSS** the remaining dressing with the arugula in a large bowl and place a little in the center of each plate of tuna. Top with the Parmesan shavings and serve.

ASPARAGUS WITH BALSAMIC VINEGAR AND PARMESAN

ASPARAGI CON ACETO BALSAMICO E PARMIGIANO

SERVES 4   PREPARATION TIME: 20 MINUTES   COOKING TIME: 12 MINUTES

The addition of balsamic vinegar and Parmesan cheese really brings out the depth of flavor in the asparagus.

1 pound fresh **asparagus**, trimmed

2 tablespoons **extra-virgin olive oil**

2 tablespoons **balsamic vinegar** *(see page 10)*

2 tablespoons **Parmesan cheese** shavings

freshly ground **black pepper**

1 **HEAT** the oven to 425°F.

2 **TOSS** the asparagus with 1 tablespoon of the extra-virgin olive oil and place on a baking sheet that has been lined with parchment paper. Bake in the hot oven 10 to 12 minutes until the asparagus is just tender. Remove from the oven.

3 **PLACE** the asparagus on a serving dish and drizzle over the balsamic vinegar and remaining olive oil. Top with the Parmesan shavings and freshly ground black pepper to taste. Serve warm.

PIEDMONT ROAST BELL PEPPERS

PEPERONI ARROSTI ALLA PIEMONTESE

SERVES **4** PREPARATION TIME: **15** MINUTES COOKING TIME: **35** MINUTES

These peppers are full of tangy flavors and they also look spectacular.

---

4 red bell peppers, halved lengthwise

½ pound cherry tomatoes

16 stuffed green olives

8 anchovy fillets, rinsed

1 clove garlic, very thinly sliced

1 tablespoon capers, rinsed

3 tablespoons butter

2 tablespoons extra-virgin olive oil

1 small handful fresh basil, roughly chopped

1 **HEAT** the oven to 400°F.

2 **REMOVE** all the membranes and seeds from the halved bell peppers and arrange them on a lightly greased baking sheet, cut side up.

3 **DIVIDE** the cherry tomatoes, olives, anchovy fillets, garlic, and capers evenly between each bell pepper half. Top each with a small knob of butter and drizzle over the extra-virgin olive oil.

4 **BAKE** in the hot oven 30 to 35 minutes until the peppers are soft but still hold their shape. Leave to cool about 5 minutes, then sprinkle over the fresh basil and serve.

ZUCCHINI FRITTATA

FRITTATA CON LE ZUCCHINE

SERVES 4　PREPARATION TIME: 15 MINUTES　COOKING TIME: 10 MINUTES

The eggs should be cooked until they are just beginning to set. This will give the dish a lovely creamy consistency and allow the full flavor of the other ingredients to shine through.

---

2 tablespoons **butter**

1 **onion**, diced

2 **zucchinis**, diced

2 **potatoes**, peeled, cooked, and cut into small chunks

5 **eggs**

1 large handful **flat-leaf parsley**, chopped

1 small handful **basil leaves**, shredded

6 tablespoons freshly grated **Parmesan cheese**

salt and freshly ground **black pepper**

1 MELT the butter in a large, non-stick skillet. Add the onion and cook over a very low heat 2 to 3 minutes until soft but not brown.

2 ADD the diced zucchinis and cook another 2 to 3 minutes until just soft, then add the potatoes, and cook a further 1 minute.

3 BEAT together the eggs, parsley, basil, and Parmesan cheese in a large bowl and season to taste with salt and pepper. Pour over the vegetable mixture in the pan and leave to cook over a low heat around 5 minutes until the egg mixture has set around the sides but is still liquid in the center, then remove from the heat. Meanwhile, heat the broiler until very hot.

4 PLACE the frittata, still in the skillet, under the hot broiler briefly to brown the top. Serve warm or cold, cut into 4 individual portions.

ANCHOVY AND GARLIC DIP

BAGNA CAUDA

SERVES 4 PREPARATION TIME: 30 MINUTES COOKING TIME: 5 MINUTES

This warm dip is deliciously salty and tastes terrific with freshly prepared vegetable crudités.

⅔ cup **olive oil**

6 cloves **garlic**, crushed

4 ounces **anchovy** fillets, finely chopped

1 stick **butter**, diced

assorted **vegetable crudités**, such as sticks of carrots and celery, trimmed radishes, and small flowerets of blanched broccoli, freshly prepared

1 **WARM** the olive oil, garlic, and anchovies in a small saucepan over a low heat, stirring well to combine. Leave to cook 4 to 5 minutes, stirring occasionally, until the anchovies form a paste, but do not allow the garlic to brown.

2 **REMOVE** from the heat and stir in the butter until it has melted.

3 **POUR** the dip into a bowl and serve warm with the fresh crudités.

WILD MUSHROOM AND SHALLOT TARTS

TORTE DI FUNGHI E SCALOGNO

SERVES 4   PREPARATION TIME: 45 MINUTES   COOKING TIME: 10 MINUTES

The richness of the mushrooms and the crispness of the pastry make a heavenly match.

1½ cups **all-purpose flour**

4 tablespoons freshly grated **Parmesan cheese**

salt and freshly ground **black pepper**

½ stick **butter**, diced

1 **egg yolk**

3 tablespoons **olive oil**

8 **shallots**, finely chopped

1 **red onion**, diced

¼ pound **pancetta**, diced

1 clove **garlic**, crushed

14 ounces mixed **wild mushrooms**, sliced

½ cup **red wine**

1 large handful **flat-leaf parsley**, chopped

2 handfuls **arugula**

1 **MIX** the flour, Parmesan cheese, and black pepper to taste in a large bowl. Rub in two-thirds of the butter with your fingertips until the mixture resembles fine breadcrumbs. Mix in the egg yolk with enough cold water to form a soft ball of pastry.

2 **ROLL** out and use to line 4 x 4-inch tartlet molds. Place a piece of parchment paper in each and top with a handful of baking beans. Chill in the fridge 30 minutes. Heat the oven to 400°F.

3 **BAKE** the tart shells in the hot oven about 15 minutes until starting to brown. Remove the paper and baking beans, then bake a further 10 minutes until golden. Turn out of the molds and set aside.

4 **HEAT** the oil in a large skillet. Add the shallots and cook until lightly browned. Remove from the pan and set aside. Add the onion and sauté 2 to 3 minutes until soft. Toss in the pancetta and garlic and cook 2 minutes, then add the mushrooms and cook 3 minutes. Return the shallots to the pan with the wine and allow to bubble briefly. Whisk in the remaining butter and the parsley and season to taste with salt and pepper.

5 **WARM** the tart shells in the oven. Divide the mushroom mixture among them and serve immediately with a garnish of arugula.

DEEP-FRIED RICE BALLS

SUPPLÌ

**MAKES 20   PREPARATION TIME: 40 MINUTES, PLUS 1 HOUR COOLING TIME
COOKING TIME: 10 MINUTES**

*The crisp, outer coating of these warm rice balls makes a lovely contrast
to their soft, creamy center.*

---

4 cups **chicken** or
   vegetable stock *(see page 18 or 19)*

2 tablespoons **butter**

1 clove **garlic**, crushed

1¼ cups **risotto rice** *(see page 14)*

5 tablespoons **heavy cream**

¼ cup freshly grated **Parmesan cheese**

salt and freshly ground **black pepper**

½ pound **mozzarella cheese**, cut into
   approximately 20 small cubes

2 **eggs**, lightly beaten

breadcrumbs, for coating

vegetable oil, for deep-frying

1 recipe quantity **fresh tomato sauce**
   (see page 23), **to serve**

1 **HEAT** the stock in a large pan until just beginning to bubble. Lower
the heat and keep at a low simmer.

2 **MELT** the butter in a medium saucepan over a low heat. Add the
garlic and cook 1 minute. Add the risotto rice and cook, stirring, for a
further minute. Add a ladleful of the hot stock and continue cooking,
stirring constantly, until it has been absorbed. Continue adding the
stock in this way until the rice is tender. (It may not be necessary to
add all the stock.) As soon as the rice is cooked, stir in the cream.

3 **REMOVE** from the heat, stir in the Parmesan cheese and season
to taste with salt and pepper. Spread out on a baking sheet and
leave to cool.

4 **SHAPE** spoonfuls of the cold rice mixture into balls, large enough
to encase a cube of the mozzarella, placed in the center. Roll each
ball in the beaten egg, then in the breadcrumbs, until well coated.

5 **POUR** enough oil into a pan to deep-fry the rice balls. Heat until hot
enough to brown a cube of day-old bread in about 30 seconds. Deep-fry
the prepared rice balls, in batches of 4 to 5 until crisp and golden. Drain
on paper towels and serve warm with the tomato sauce for dipping.

BRUSCHETTA WITH TOMATO AND BASIL

BRUSCHETTA CON POMODORO E BASILICO

SERVES **4**   PREPARATION TIME: **20** MINUTES   COOKING TIME: **5** MINUTES

Ripe tomatoes and fresh basil create the perfect flavor combination.

8 slices **ciabatta bread**, about ½ inch thick

1 clove **garlic**, cut in half

4 tablespoons **extra-virgin olive oil**

4 **tomatoes**, finely chopped

1 small handful **basil leaves**, torn

salt and freshly ground **black pepper**

1 **TOAST** the ciabatta slices under a hot broiler until golden brown on both sides.

2 **RUB** each piece of toast all over with the cut side of the garlic while still warm, then drizzle each with a little olive oil. Put to one side.

3 **MIX** together the chopped tomatoes and torn basil in a bowl and season to taste with salt and pepper.

4 **PLACE** 1 or 2 spoonfuls of the tomato mixture on top of each piece of toast and serve.

THICK VEGETABLE SOUP WITH PESTO
MINESTRONE ALLA GENOVESE

**SERVES 4   PREPARATION TIME: 25 MINUTES, PLUS 8 HOURS SOAKING TIME
COOKING TIME: 2 HOURS**

¾ cup dried **borlotti beans**

3 tablespoons **olive oil**

1 large **onion**, sliced

2 stalks **celery**, sliced

1 **carrot**, sliced

2 cloves **garlic**, crushed

¼ pound thickly sliced **pancetta**, diced

1 tablespoon **tomato paste**

4 cups **chicken** or **vegetable stock**
   (see page 18 or 19)

3 cups canned **chopped tomatoes**

2 **potatoes**, peeled and diced

⅔ cup shelled fresh **peas**

1 **zucchini**, diced

¼ pound **green beans**, roughly chopped

1 handful **flat-leaf parsley**, roughly chopped

salt and freshly ground **black pepper**

basil pesto *(see page 24)* and freshly grated
   Parmesan cheese, to serve

1 **PLACE** the borlotti beans in a large pan. Cover with cold water and leave to soak 8 hours or overnight. Drain, rinse several times in cold water, and set aside.

2 **HEAT** the olive oil in a large saucepan over a moderate heat. Add the onion, celery, and carrot and cook 3 to 4 minutes, stirring frequently. Add the garlic and pancetta and cook another 2 minutes, then stir in the tomato paste until well combined.

3 **STIR** the drained beans into the pan of vegetables, along with the stock and the chopped tomatoes. Lower the heat and leave to simmer about 1½ hours until the borlotti beans begin to soften.

4 **ADD** the potatoes, peas, zucchini, green beans, and parsley and continue to simmer a further 30 minutes until the vegetables are tender.

5 **SEASON** to taste with salt and freshly ground pepper and serve in warm bowls, with a spoonful of pesto and a sprinkling of freshly grated Parmesan cheese added just before serving.

VENETIAN PEA AND RICE SOUP

RISI E BISI

SERVES 4   PREPARATION TIME: 20 MINUTES   COOKING TIME: 20 MINUTES

This is a cross between a thick soup and a risotto. You could almost think of it as a "lazy" risotto, since it does not require constant stirring.

---

4 cups **chicken** or
   vegetable stock *(see page 18 or 19)*

2 tablespoons **olive oil**

½ stick **butter**

1 small **onion**, diced

2 ounces thickly sliced **pancetta**, diced

¾ cup **risotto rice** *(see page 14)*

2 cups shelled fresh **peas**

1 small handful fresh **mint**, roughly chopped

4 tablespoons freshly grated
   Parmesan cheese

salt and freshly ground **black pepper**

1 **HEAT** the stock in a saucepan until just bubbling. Keep at a gentle simmer. In a large, clean skillet heat the olive oil with half the butter. Add the onion and cook over a low heat about 5 minutes, stirring often, until soft and translucent.

2 **ADD** the pancetta and cook a further 2 minutes over a medium heat, then add the rice and stir to coat well with the butter mixture.

3 **POUR** in the hot stock, lower the heat, and leave to simmer about 10 minutes, stirring occasionally.

4 **ADD** the peas and cook a further 5 to 6 minutes until they are tender. Remove from the heat, then stir in the remaining butter, the mint, and the Parmesan cheese. Season to taste with salt and pepper and serve immediately.

WINTER VEGETABLE SOUP

LA RIBOLLITA

SERVES 4   PREPARATION TIME: 20 MINUTES   COOKING TIME: 30 MINUTES

This soup is rich and satisfying—just perfect for a midwinter treat.

---

3 tablespoons **olive oil**

1 **onion**, diced

1 large **carrot**, diced

2 stalks **celery**, diced

3 **zucchinis**, diced

2 cloves **garlic**, crushed

5 cups **chicken** or **vegetable stock** *(see page 18 or 19)*

¾ pound **cavolo nero**, finely sliced *(see page 15)*

4 cups fresh **white breadcrumbs**

salt and freshly ground **black pepper**

extra-virgin olive oil, to serve

1 **HEAT** the olive oil in a large saucepan. Add the onion and cook over a low heat 2 to 3 minutes, until soft. Add the carrot, celery, and zucchinis and cook a further 5 minutes, then stir in the garlic and cook another minute.

2 **ADD** the stock and cavolo nero and bring to a boil. Lower the heat, stir in the breadcrumbs, and leave to simmer gently around 30 minutes until the vegetables are tender.

3 **SEASON** to taste with salt and pepper. Serve in warm bowls with a little extra-virgin olive oil drizzled over the top.

FISH SOUP

ZUPPA DI PESCE

SERVES 4 PREPARATION TIME: 25 MINUTES COOKING TIME: 30 MINUTES

This intensely flavored seafood broth is light and refreshing.

½ pound raw jumbo **shrimp**, shelled

6 ounces **monkfish** fillets, membrane removed

6 ounces **cod**

6 ounces **scallops**

3 tablespoons **olive oil**

1 small stalk **celery**, finely diced

1 **carrot**, finely diced

1 bulb **fennel**, finely diced

2 cloves **garlic**, crushed

⅔ cup dry **white wine**

3 cups canned **chopped tomatoes**

4 cups **fish stock** *(see page 19)*

salt and freshly ground **black pepper**

1 handful **flat-leaf parsley**, roughly chopped

1 **PEEL** the shrimp and cut the monkfish, cod, and scallops into bite-size pieces. Set aside in the fridge until required.

2 **HEAT** the oil in a large saucepan. Add the celery, carrot, and fennel and cook over a medium heat around 5 minutes, stirring often to prevent browning. Add the garlic and cook another 1 minute.

3 **POUR** in the white wine, chopped tomatoes, and fish stock and bring to a boil. Reduce the heat and leave to simmer 25 minutes.

4 **STIR** in the prepared fish and continue to simmer a further 5 minutes. Season to taste with salt and pepper and stir in the chopped parsley. Serve immediately.

PASTA AND BEAN SOUP

PASTA E FAGIOLI

**SERVES 4   PREPARATION TIME: 20 MINUTES, PLUS 8 HOURS SOAKING TIME
COOKING TIME: 1½ HOURS**

*This is a typical rustic Italian soup. The swirl of olive oil, added on the
top just before serving, helps to enhance the flavor.*

1½ cups dried **borlotti beans**

2 sprigs fresh **rosemary**

1 tablespoon **olive oil**

1 **onion**, diced

2 cloves **garlic**, peeled

6 cups **chicken** or
   vegetable stock *(see page 18 or 19)*

2 handfuls **flat-leaf parsley**, roughly chopped

salt and freshly ground **black pepper**

4 ounces short **pasta tubes**

extra-virgin olive oil, to serve

1 **PLACE** the borlotti beans in a large pan. Cover with cold water and leave to soak 8 hours or overnight.

2 **DRAIN** the beans and rinse thoroughly. Place in a clean pan and cover with plenty of fresh cold water. Add the rosemary and bring to a boil. Simmer about 1 hour or until tender. Drain and put to one side.

3 **HEAT** the olive oil in a clean pan, add the onion, and cook about 5 minutes on a very low heat, stirring occasionally. Add the garlic and cook another minute.

4 **ADD** the drained beans to the pan with the stock and about two-thirds of the parsley and season to taste with salt and pepper. Bring to a boil, lower the heat, and leave to simmer 30 minutes. Allow to cool a little.

5 **TRANSFER** to a blender or food processor and process until smooth (or use an immersion blender—see page 16). Return to the cleaned pan, add the pasta, and cook 10 to 12 minutes or until the pasta is tender. Season, if necessary, with salt and pepper.

6 **DIVIDE** among warm serving bowls, and serve, topped with a swirl of extra-virgin olive oil and a sprinkling of the remaining parsley.

CREAMY TOMATO SOUP

PAPPA AL POMODORO

SERVES 4   PREPARATION TIME: 20 MINUTES   COOKING TIME: 5 MINUTES

This creamy tomato soup, with its vibrant flavour, originates in Tuscany. It is often served as a very thick, almost stew-like soup, although this version is much lighter.

3 tablespoons **olive oil**

1 **onion**, sliced

2 cloves **garlic**, chopped

1¼ pound ripe **tomatoes**, peeled, deseeded, and chopped

4 tablespoons fresh **white breadcrumbs**

1 small handful fresh **basil leaves**, torn

2 cups **chicken stock** *(see page 18)*

salt and freshly ground **black pepper**

1 **HEAT** the olive oil in a medium-sized saucepan. Add the onion and cook over a very low heat 2 to 3 minutes, until soft. Add the garlic and cook for another minute.

2 **STIR** in the tomatoes and cook gently about 3 minutes.

3 **REMOVE** from the heat and allow to cool slightly. Add the fresh breadcrumbs, basil, and stock and transfer to a blender or food processor and process until smooth (or use an immersion blender, see page 16).

4 **RETURN** to the cleaned pan and heat through. Season to taste with salt and pepper and serve.

SPAGHETTI WITH PRAWNS

SPAGHETTI CON GAMBERETTI

SERVES 4 PREPARATION TIME: 10 MINUTES COOKING TIME: 12 MINUTES

This simple yet elegant pasta dish is quick to prepare and packed with flavor.

---

14 ounces dried **spaghetti**

2 tablespoons **extra-virgin olive oil**

2 tablespoons **butter**

1 small **onion**, finely diced

¾ pound raw **shrimp**, shelled

3 **tomatoes**, diced

½ cup dry **white wine**

salt and freshly ground **black pepper**

1 small handful fresh **basil leaves**, torn

1 **BRING** a large pan of salted water to a boil. Add the spaghetti and cook, according to the package instructions until tender. Drain.

2 **HEAT** the olive oil and butter in another large saucepan while the pasta is cooking. Add the onion and cook, stirring frequently, about 5 minutes until soft.

3 **ADD** the shrimp to the softened onion and continue cooking until they start to turn pink. Stir in the tomatoes and white wine, then season to taste with salt and pepper.

4 **TOSS** the shrimp mixture and the basil with the freshly cooked pasta, until well mixed. Adjust the seasoning if needed and serve immediately.

SPAGHETTI WITH BREADCRUMBS

SPAGHETTI CON LA MOLLICA

SERVES **4**   PREPARATION TIME: **10** MINUTES   COOKING TIME: **12** MINUTES

*The crunch of the breadcrumbs lends a surprising touch to this dish
and adds a truly satisfying dimension to every mouthful.*

⅓ cup **olive oil**

3½ ounces **anchovies**, rinsed and drained

2 cloves **garlic**, crushed

1½ cups fresh **white breadcrumbs**

14 ounces dried **spaghetti**

5 tablespoons pitted **black olives**, sliced

1 tablespoon **capers**, rinsed

juice and grated zest of 1 **lemon**

freshly ground **black pepper**

1 **HEAT** 2 tablespoons of olive oil in a small saucepan. Add the anchovies and cook until they form a paste. Add the garlic and cook for another minute. Put to one side.

2 **HEAT** the remaining oil in a large skillet. Add the breadcrumbs and stir well to combine with the oil, then continue to cook until the breadcrumbs become golden brown. Remove from the heat and set aside.

3 **COOK** the spaghetti, according to the package instructions, until tender, and drain.

4 **MIX** the freshly cooked pasta, the anchovy paste, breadcrumbs, olives, capers, and lemon juice and zest. Season to taste with black pepper and serve immediately.

RIGATONI WITH ROASTED VEGETABLES

RIGATONI CON VERDURE ARROSTITE

SERVES 4 PREPARATION TIME: 15 MINUTES COOKING TIME: 40 MINUTES

The combination of roasted vegetables, fresh Parmesan, and warm pasta makes a spectacular dish, fit for anything from a simple lunch to opener for a special dinner.

2 **carrots**, peeled

6 ounces **pumpkin**, peeled

2 **sweet potatoes**, peeled

1 **parsnip**, peeled

2 **zucchinis**

5 tablespoons **olive oil**

2 cloves **garlic**, sliced finely

1 small **chili**, deseeded and finely diced

2 sprigs **rosemary**, roughly chopped

salt and freshly ground **black pepper**

½ pound **cherry tomatoes**

14 ounces dried **rigatoni pasta**

2 tablespoons **extra-virgin olive oil**

1 large handful **flat-leaf parsley**, chopped

freshly grated **Parmesan cheese**, to serve

1 HEAT the oven to 350°F.

2 CUT the vegetables into roughly bite-size chunks, making the carrots just a little smaller than the other vegetables. Place in a large bowl.

3 TOSS in the olive oil, garlic, chili, and rosemary, then season to taste with salt and pepper. Mix well until the vegetables are thoroughly coated in the seasoned oil. Arrange in a single layer on a baking sheet.

4 ROAST the vegetables in the hot oven about 20 minutes until just starting to become tender. Add the tomatoes and cook a further 10 minutes until all the vegetables are cooked.

5 COOK the rigatoni in plenty of boiling salted water, according to the package instructions, then drain.

6 TOSS the freshly cooked pasta with the extra-virgin olive oil, freshly roasted vegetables, and chopped parsley. Serve immediately, sprinkled with freshly grated Parmesan cheese.

THREE CHEESE RAVIOLI WITH BUTTER AND BASIL *RAVIOLI AI TRE FORMAGGI CON BURRO E BASILICO*

SERVES **4** PREPARATION TIME: **40** MINUTES COOKING TIME: **10** MINUTES

The delicate flavor of these light pasta packages is enhanced by the addition of extra-virgin olive oil, fragrant fresh basil, and a dash of mouth-tingling lemon.

½ pound **ricotta cheese**

⅓ cup freshly grated **pecorino cheese**

⅓ cup freshly grated **Parmesan cheese**, plus extra for serving

1 small handful fresh **basil leaves**, shredded, plus extra for serving

salt and freshly ground **black pepper**

1 recipe quantity **fresh pasta** dough *(see page 26)*

1 tablespoon **olive oil**

3 tablespoons **extra-virgin olive oil**

2 tablespoons **butter**, melted

juice and grated zest of 1 **lemon**

1 **MIX** the ricotta, pecorino, and Parmesan cheeses with the basil in a bowl. Season with a little salt and plenty of pepper and set aside.

2 **CUT** the pasta dough into 4 pieces and roll out each one up to the second thinnest setting on the pasta machine. Lay 1 sheet of pasta on a well-floured surface and place 12 heaped teaspoons of the cheese mixture at equal intervals along it, allowing enough space around each to seal the ravioli. Brush around each heap of cheese mixture with a little water.

3 **PLACE** a second pasta sheet on top. Press down gently around the heaps of cheese filling to seal the 2 sheets of pasta together, making sure no excess air is trapped around the filling. With a sharp knife, cut into 12 individual ravioli. Repeat this process with the remaining 2 sheets of pasta to prepare 12 more ravioli.

4 **BOIL** a large saucepan of salted water. Add the tablespoon of olive oil, then the ravioli, and cook about 5 minutes until the pasta is tender but still has some bite. Carefully lift out of the water and drain using a slotted spoon. Divide among 4 warm serving plates.

5 **MIX** together the extra-virgin olive oil, melted butter, and lemon juice and zest in a bowl and season to taste with pepper. Drizzle over the ravioli and serve with a sprinkling of shredded basil and grated Parmesan.

TAGLIATELLE WITH ASPARAGUS

TAGLIATELLE CON ASPARAGI

SERVES 4   PREPARATION TIME: 20 MINUTES   COOKING TIME: 12 MINUTES

The heat from the chili helps to bring out all the flavors in this fabulous pasta dish.

---

1 pound fresh **asparagus**, trimmed

1 tablespoon **olive oil**

1 small **onion**, diced

1 clove **garlic**, crushed

1 **red chili**, deseeded and finely diced

3 **tomatoes**, peeled, deseeded, and chopped

⅓ cup dry **white wine**

1 small handful **basil leaves**, shredded

1 large handful **flat-leaf parsley**, chopped

salt and freshly ground **black pepper**

14 ounces fresh or dried **tagliatelle** *(see page 14)*

freshly grated **Parmesan cheese**, to serve

1 **PLUNGE** the asparagus into a pan of boiling water 1 minute, then drain, and rinse thoroughly under cold running water to cool. Cut into approximately ½ inch lengths on the diagonal and put to one side.

2 **HEAT** the olive oil in a large sauté pan (see page 17). Add the onion and cook over a medium heat 3 to 5 minutes until soft and slightly golden. Add the asparagus, garlic, and chili and continue cooking for another 3 to 4 minutes.

3 **POUR** in the tomatoes and white wine and bring to a boil. Lower the heat and simmer gently 5 minutes. Stir in the basil and parsley. Season to taste with salt and pepper, then set aside, and keep warm.

4 **COOK** the pasta in a large pan of boiling salted water until just tender. Drain, then toss with the warm sauce and serve, sprinkled with freshly grated Parmesan cheese.

"ANGRY" PASTA

PENNE ALL'ARRABBIATA

SERVES 4   PREPARATION TIME: 15 MINUTES   COOKING TIME: 20 MINUTES

This dish is typically served very hot and spicy, hence its name. But you can make it as mild or as fiery as you prefer by increasing or decreasing the number of chilies you use when preparing the sauce.

---

2 tablespoons **olive oil**

1 **onion**, sliced

2 **red chilies**, deseeded and finely diced

½ pound thickly sliced **pancetta**, diced

1 clove **garlic**, crushed

6 cups canned **chopped tomatoes**

⅓ cup dry **white wine**

14 ounces dried **penne pasta**

1 handful **flat-leaf parsley**, chopped roughly

freshly shaved or grated **Parmesan cheese**, for serving

1 **HEAT** the oil in a large sauté pan (see page 17). Add the onion and cook over a moderate heat 3 minutes, stirring often to prevent browning. Add the chili, pancetta, and garlic and continue cooking for another 2 minutes.

2 **STIR** in the tomatoes and white wine. Lower the heat and leave to simmer 15 minutes, until the sauce has thickened. Put to one side and keep warm.

3 **COOK** the penne in plenty of boiling salted water, according to the package instructions until it is tender but still retains some bite. Drain and toss with the warm sauce and the chopped parsley. Serve with the freshly shaved or grated Parmesan.

BAKED LASAGNE

LASAGNE AL FORNO

SERVES 4 TO 6   PREPARATION TIME: 35 MINUTES, PLUS 2 TO 3 HOURS
COOKING TIME FOR SAUCE   COOKING TIME: 40 TO 45 MINUTES

Nothing beats the flavor of a traditional, homemade lasagne. The layers should be distinct and oozing with rich warming ragù sauce and creamy béchamel.

---

4 tablespoons olive oil

1 onion, diced

1 carrot, finely diced

2 stalks celery, finely diced

¼ pound thickly sliced pancetta, diced

1 pound lean ground beef

1 pound ground veal

1 cup milk

1 cup white wine

3 cups canned chopped tomatoes

3 cups passata *(see page 14)*

2 cups water

salt and freshly ground black pepper

1 recipe quantity fresh pasta sheets *(see page 26)*

1 recipe quantity béchamel sauce *(see page 20)*

4 tablespoons freshly grated
  Parmesan cheese

1 HEAT the olive oil in a large pan over a low heat. Add the onion and cook 2 to 3 minutes until soft. Add the carrot and celery, and cook another 2 minutes.

2 TURN up the heat, add the pancetta, and cook, stirring, 1 minute. Add the beef and veal and cook until the meat is brown. Pour in the milk and allow to boil vigorously until all the liquid evaporates.

3 ADD the wine, tomatoes, and passata and turn the heat down to very low. Pour in the water and season to taste with salt and pepper. Simmer very gently about 2 to 3 hours to let the flavors fully develop, adding extra water if required to prevent the sauce becoming too dry. Put to one side to cool until needed. Heat the oven to 350°F.

4 CUT the fresh pasta sheets into pieces that will fit the base of an ovenproof dish, approximately 10½ inches by 8 inches. Layer the pasta with the meat sauce and béchamel sauce into the dish, starting with a layer of pasta and ending with a layer of béchamel. Sprinkle the Parmesan cheese over the top.

5 BAKE in the hot oven 40 to 45 minutes, until lightly browned and bubbling. Serve.

SPAGHETTI CARBONARA

SPAGHETTI ALLA CARBONARA

SERVES 4   PREPARATION TIME: 10 MINUTES   COOKING TIME: 12 MINUTES

This perennially popular recipe originated in the Lazio region of Italy, which has Rome at its center, but it can now be found all over Italy.

2 **eggs**

2 tablespoons freshly grated **Parmesan cheese**

2 tablespoons freshly grated **pecorino cheese**

1 tablespoon **olive oil**

2 tablespoons **butter**

1 clove **garlic**, crushed

6 ounces thickly sliced **pancetta**, diced

14 ounces dried **spaghetti**

salt and freshly ground **black pepper**

1 **WHISK** together the eggs, Parmesan, and pecorino in a bowl and set on one side.

2 **HEAT** the olive oil and butter in a skillet. Add the garlic and pancetta and cook over a medium heat until the pancetta is crisp and the garlic is golden brown. Discard the garlic and put the pancetta to one side.

3 **COOK** the spaghetti in plenty of salted boiling water, according to the instructions on the package, until tender but still retaining some bite.

4 **DRAIN** the pasta, then return it to the pan. Toss in the egg mixture and the cooked pancetta and combine well. Season to taste with salt and pepper and serve immediately, with extra grated Parmesan sprinkled over the top if desired.

SPINACH AND RICOTTA RAVIOLI

RAVIOLI DI RICOTTA E SPINACI

SERVES 4   PREPARATION TIME: 40 MINUTES   COOKING TIME: 10 MINUTES

With their subtle flavorings of ricotta cheese, spinach, and nutmeg, these traditional ravioli are mouth-wateringly delicious.

---

1 pound fresh **spinach**, rinsed thoroughly

2 tablespoons **butter**

1 small **onion**, diced

2 tablespoons freshly grated **Parmesan cheese**, plus extra for serving

½ pound **ricotta cheese**

½ teaspoon freshly grated **nutmeg**

salt and freshly ground **black pepper**

1 recipe quantity **fresh pasta** dough *(see page 26)*

¾ stick **butter**, melted

1 **COOK** the spinach in a small amount of boiling water until just wilted. Drain, squeeze out as much water as possible, chop finely, and set aside.

2 **MELT** the butter in a pan over a low heat. Add the onion and cook 3-4 minutes until soft. Off the heat, stir in the spinach, Parmesan, ricotta, and nutmeg. Season to taste with salt and pepper and set aside.

3 **CUT** the pasta dough into 4 pieces and roll out each one up to the second thinnest setting on the pasta machine. Lay 1 pasta sheet on a floured surface and place 12 heaped teaspoons of the spinach mixture at equal intervals along it, allowing enough space around each to seal the ravioli. Brush around each heap of spinach mixture with a little water.

4 **PLACE** a second pasta sheet on top. Press down gently around the heaps of filling to seal the 2 sheets of pasta together, insuring no excess air is trapped around the filling. With a sharp knife, cut into 12 individual ravioli. Repeat with the remaining pasta sheets and filling.

5 **BOIL** a large saucepan of salted water. Add the ravioli and cook 5 minutes, or until the pasta is just tender. Lift out of the pan and drain, using a slotted spoon, then divide among 4 warm serving plates.

6 **DRIZZLE** the melted butter over the top of the ravioli, sprinkle with some freshly grated Parmesan cheese, and serve.

POTATO GNOCCHI WITH BASIL, MOZZARELLA, AND ROASTED CHERRY TOMATOES *GNOCCHI DI PATATE*

SERVES 4   PREPARATION TIME: 40 MINUTES   COOKING TIME: 5 MINUTES

Using a potato ricer will produce the lightest possible gnocchi. If you do not have one, however, you can simply mash them.

½ pound **cherry tomatoes**

1 tablespoon **olive oil**

2 pounds **potatoes**, wrapped in foil and baked in the oven until very soft

2 cups all-purpose **flour**

1 **egg**, lightly beaten

salt and freshly ground **black pepper**

3 tablespoons **basil pesto** (*see page 24*)

1 small handful baby **mozzarella cheeses**, halved

freshly grated **Parmesan cheese**, to serve

1 **HEAT** the oven to 400°F. Arrange the cherry tomatoes on a baking sheet, sprinkle over the olive oil, and cook in the hot oven until just soft. Set on one side.

2 **SCOOP** the flesh out of the potatoes, discarding the skins, and press through a potato ricer (or simply mash). Place in a large bowl with the flour and egg and stir to combine. Season to taste with salt and pepper, then tip onto a floured surface, and knead to form a soft, pliable dough.

3 **SHAPE** the dough into long cylinders approximately ⅔ inch in diameter, then cut each one into ¾ inch lengths. Mark these gnocchi lengths lightly with the back of a fork, then arrange on a tray that has been lightly dusted with flour.

4 **BRING** a large pan of salted water to a boil. Add the gnocchi and cook about 5 minutes, or until the gnocchi rise to the top of the water. Lift out of the pan and drain, using a slotted spoon.

5 **PLACE** the hot gnocchi in a large bowl with the pesto, mozzarella, and cherry tomatoes and toss gently to combine. Serve immediately, sprinkled with freshly grated Parmesan cheese.

SEMOLINA GNOCCHI WITH FRESH TOMATO SAUCE

GNOCCHI ALLA ROMANA

SERVES 4 TO 6   PREPARATION TIME: 20 MINUTES, PLUS 1 HOUR COOLING TIME COOKING TIME: 20 MINUTES

This is real comfort food. Just serve with a simple green salad.

---

4 cups **milk**

salt and freshly ground **black pepper**

1 cup **semolina**

2 **egg yolks**

½ pound **Parmesan cheese**, freshly grated

½ stick **butter**, chopped

1 recipe quantity **fresh tomato sauce**
  (see page 23)

1 **HEAT** the milk in a saucepan with a little salt and pepper until it is just starting to boil.

2 **WHISK** in the semolina, then cook about 10 minutes over a low heat, stirring constantly with a wooden spoon, until the mixture becomes quite thick.

3 **REMOVE** from the heat and add the egg yolks, half the Parmesan cheese, and half the butter.

4 **SPREAD** the mixture over a large baking sheet lined with wax paper, to a depth of about ½ inch. Leave to cool 1 hour.

5 **HEAT** the oven to 400°F. Grease an ovenproof dish with a little of the remaining butter.

6 **CUT** circles out from the cooled gnocchi mixture, using a cookie cutter, and arrange in a single layer in the greased dish. Dot with the remaining butter. Spoon over the tomato sauce and sprinkle over the remaining Parmesan cheese.

7 **BAKE** the gnocchi in the hot oven about 20 minutes until golden brown and bubbling. Serve immediately.

SAFFRON RISOTTO

RISOTTO ALLA MILANESE

SERVES 4   PREPARATION TIME: 10 MINUTES   COOKING TIME: 20 MINUTES

The saffron gives this risotto a rich yellow color and intense flavor.

4 cups **chicken** or
  vegetable stock *(see page 18 or 19)*

¾ stick **butter**

1 small **onion**, diced

1½ cups **risotto rice** *(see page 14)*

½ cup **white wine**

¼ teaspoon **saffron threads**, soaked in
  2 tablespoons boiling water for 10 minutes,
  water reserved

4 tablespoons freshly grated **Parmesan cheese**,
  plus extra for serving

salt and freshly ground **black pepper**

1 **HEAT** the stock over a medium heat until just beginning to boil. Lower the heat and leave to simmer very gently.

2 **MELT** ½ stick butter in another saucepan. Add the onion and cook over a low heat around 5 minutes until soft but not brown.

3 **ADD** the rice and toast for 2 minutes, stirring constantly, then add the white wine and stir until it has evaporated. Add a ladleful of the hot stock and cook, stirring constantly, until it has all been absorbed by the rice. Continue in this way, adding the saffron and its soaking liquid after the first 10 minutes of cooking, until the rice is just tender but still retains some bite and is creamy in consistency. (It may not be necessary to use all the stock.)

4 **STIR** in the remaining butter and the Parmesan cheese and season to taste with salt and pepper. Leave to stand, covered, 1 to 2 minutes, then serve with extra freshly grated Parmesan cheese.

ASPARAGUS RISOTTO

RISOTTO CON ASPARAGI

SERVES 4   PREPARATION TIME: 10 MINUTES   COOKING TIME: 20 MINUTES

The freshness of the asparagus combines superbly with the creaminess of the risotto rice in this truly sublime dish.

1 pound **green asparagus**, trimmed

4 cups **chicken** or **vegetable stock**
(*see page 18 or 19*)

¾ stick **butter**

1 small **onion**, finely diced

1½ cups **risotto rice** (*see page 14*)

4 tablespoons freshly grated **Parmesan cheese**, plus extra for serving (optional)

salt and freshly ground **black pepper**

1 COOK the asparagus in a pan of boiling salted water until just starting to soften. Drain, rinse under cold running water to cool, then pat dry on paper towels. Cut into bite-size chunks and set on one side.

2 HEAT the stock over a medium heat until just beginning to boil. Lower the heat and leave to simmer very gently.

3 MELT ½ stick butter in another saucepan. Add the the onion and cook over a low heat 3 to 4 minutes until soft but not brown.

4 STIR in the rice and allow to toast for 2 minutes, then add a ladleful of the hot stock and cook, stirring constantly, until it has all been absorbed by the rice. Continue in this way, adding hot stock and stirring, until the rice is just tender but still retains some bite and is creamy in consistency. (It may not be necessary to use all the stock.)

5 STIR in the asparagus, the remaining butter, and the Parmesan cheese and adjust the seasoning if necessary. Leave to stand, covered, 1 to 2 minutes, then serve with extra freshly grated Parmesan cheese sprinkled over the top (optional).

MUSHROOM RISOTTO

RISOTTO AI FUNGHI

SERVES 4   PREPARATION TIME: 10 MINUTES   COOKING TIME: 20 MINUTES

Risotto makes a great meal at any time and one of the best ways of flavoring it is by cooking it with wild mushrooms.

1 pound **wild mushrooms** *(see page 12)*

1½ sticks **butter**

4 cups **chicken** or **vegetable stock** *(see page 18 or 19)*

1 small **onion**, diced

1½ cups **risotto rice** *(see page 14)*

4 tablespoons freshly grated **Parmesan cheese**, plus extra for serving (optional)

salt and freshly ground **black pepper**

1 **WIPE** the mushrooms thoroughly and slice thinly. Heat ½ stick butter in a sauté pan (see page 17) and cook the mushrooms 4 to 5 minutes until soft. Remove from the pan and set aside.

2 **HEAT** the stock over a medium heat until just beginning to boil. Lower the heat and leave to simmer very gently.

3 **MELT** ½ stick butter in another saucepan. Add the onion and cook over a low heat 3 to 4 minutes, until soft but not brown.

4 **STIR** in the rice and allow to toast for 2 minutes, then add a ladleful of the hot stock and cook, stirring constantly, until it has all been absorbed by the rice. Continue in this way, adding hot stock and stirring, until the rice is just tender but still retains some bite and is creamy in consistency. (It may not be necessary to use all the stock.)

5 **STIR** in the mushrooms, the remaining butter, and Parmesan cheese and adjust the seasoning if necessary. Leave to stand, covered, 1 to 2 minutes, then serve with extra freshly grated Parmesan cheese sprinkled over the top (optional).

RISOTTO WITH SHRIMP AND CHAMPAGNE

RISOTTO ALLO CHAMPAGNE CON GAMBERETTI

SERVES 4   PREPARATION TIME: 15 MINUTES   COOKING TIME: 20 MINUTES

Make this for a special celebration meal, or anytime you feel indulgent.

½ pound raw **shrimp**, shelled

3 cups **fish stock** *(see page 19)*

¾ stick **butter**

1 small **onion**, finely diced

1 clove **garlic**, crushed

1½ cups **risotto rice** *(see page 14)*

¾ cup **Champagne**

salt and freshly ground **black pepper**

1 **RINSE** the shrimp cut in half horizontally and keep refrigerated until required.

2 **HEAT** the stock over a medium heat until just beginning to boil. Lower the heat and leave to simmer very gently.

3 **MELT** ½ stick butter in another saucepan. Add the onion and garlic and cook over a low heat 3 to 4 minutes until soft but not brown.

4 **ADD** the rice and toast for 1 minute, stirring constantly, then pour over half of the champagne and keep stirring until it has evaporated.

5 **POUR** in a ladleful of the hot stock and cook, stirring constantly, until it has all been absorbed by the rice. Continue in this way, adding hot stock and stirring, until the rice is just tender but still retains some bite and is a creamy consistency. (It may not be necessary to use all the stock.)

6 **TOSS** in the shrimp and cook a further minute until they turn pink. Stir in the remaining Champagne and butter and season to taste with salt and pepper. Serve immediately.

BRAISED BEEF WITH RED WINE, TUSCAN-STYLE *SPEZZATINO DI MANZO ALLA TOSCANA*

SERVES 4   PREPARATION TIME: 20 MINUTES   COOKING TIME: 1½ TO 2 HOURS

The depth of flavor of this dish comes from the long cooking time. The addition of a small amount of chili cuts through and enhances the richness of the sauce and the meat is meltingly tender.

⅓ cup **olive oil**

2 pounds **beef** suitable for braising, cut into 2 inch cubes

2 **onions**, cut in half and sliced

2 cloves **garlic**, crushed

1 **red chili**, deseeded and finely chopped

2 tablespoons **tomato paste**

4 cups **beef stock** *(see page 18)*

14 ounces canned **chopped tomatoes**

1¼ cups **red wine**

4 sprigs fresh **rosemary**

6 fresh **sage leaves**, chopped

salt and freshly ground **black pepper**

1 small handful **flat-leaf parsley**, chopped

1 recipe quantity **"wet" polenta** *(see page 27)*, to serve

1 **HEAT** 3 tablespoons of the oil in a large skillet over a medium heat. Add half the beef and brown lightly on all sides. Set on one side. Repeat with the remaining beef, then set aside with the first batch.

2 **ADD** the remaining oil to the skillet and heat through. Toss in the onions, garlic, and chili and cook over a medium heat until the onions are soft and translucent.

3 **STIR** in the tomato paste and cook, still stirring, 1 minute. Pour over the beef stock, tomatoes, and red wine and stir to combine.

4 **RETURN** the meat to the skillet. Add the rosemary and sage and season to taste with salt and pepper.

5 **SIMMER** over a low heat, partially covered, 1½ to 2 hours until the beef is really tender and the sauce has thickened slightly. Check the seasoning and adjust if necessary. Serve sprinkled with the chopped parsley, accompanied by a helping of "wet" polenta.

MEATBALLS WITH TOMATO SAUCE AND CRUSTY BREAD

POLPETTE AL SUGO

SERVES 4 PREPARATION TIME: 35 MINUTES COOKING TIME: 45 MINUTES

This delicious mix of lightly spiced meatballs, fresh tomato sauce, and melted cheese will leave you using the bread to mop up every last drop of juice.

---

1 pound ground **beef**

1 pound ground **veal**

1 **onion**, finely diced

3 tablespoons fresh **white breadcrumbs**

1 large handful **flat-leaf parsley**, chopped

leaves from a small handful fresh **rosemary sprigs**, chopped

1 **egg**

salt and freshly ground **black pepper**

2 tablespoons **olive oil**

1 recipe quantity **fresh tomato sauce** *(see page 23)*

1 ball **mozzarella cheese**, freshly grated

8 tablespoons freshly grated **Parmesan cheese**

1 small handful fresh **basil leaves**, torn

1 loaf crusty **bread**

1 **HEAT** the oven to 350°F.

2 **MIX** together the ground beef, ground veal, onion, breadcrumbs, parsley, rosemary, and egg in a large bowl. Season to taste with salt and pepper.

3 **ROLL** the meat mixture into small, bite-size balls and put to one side.

4 **HEAT** the oil in a large non-stick frying pan over a medium heat. Add half the meatballs and cook until lightly brown all over. Remove from the pan and set aside. Repeat with the remaining meatballs and set aside with the first batch. Transfer all the meatballs to a casserole dish large enough to hold them in 1 layer.

5 **POUR** the tomato sauce over the top of the meatballs and sprinkle over the grated mozzarella and Parmesan cheeses. Bake in the hot oven about 45 minutes until the cheese is lightly browned and the sauce is bubbling. Stir in the torn basil leaves (or reserve, and scatter over) and serve immediately, accompanied by the crusty bread.

VEAL SHANKS WITH WHITE WINE

OSSO BUCO ALLA MILANESE

SERVES **4**   PREPARATION TIME: **30** MINUTES   COOKING TIME: **2** HOURS

This hearty casserole is ideal for serving up on a frosty winter night.

---

4 x 1¼ inch thick, center-cut slices **veal** shin

1½ cups **flour**, seasoned with **salt** and freshly ground **black pepper**

8 tablespoons **olive oil**

2 tablespoons **butter**

1 **onion**, diced

1 **carrot**, diced

1 stalk **celery**, diced

2 cloves **garlic**, crushed

2 **bay leaves**

3 sprigs fresh **thyme**

1 cup dry **white wine**

3 cups canned **chopped tomatoes**

1 cup **beef stock** *(see page 18)*

1 recipe quantity **saffron risotto** *(see page 94)*, to serve

1 **HEAT** the oven to 325°F.

2 **ROLL** the veal pieces in the seasoned flour until lightly coated and set on one side. Heat 4 tablespoons of the oil in a large sauté pan (see page 17) over a medium heat. Add the veal and brown lightly on all sides. Transfer to a large, ovenproof casserole dish.

3 **WIPE** the sauté pan clean and add the remaining oil with the butter. Place over a very low heat until the butter has melted. Toss in the onion and cook 3 to 4 minutes until soft but not brown, then add the carrot, celery, and garlic and cook a further 3 to 4 minutes.

4 **STIR** in the bay leaves, thyme, white wine, tomatoes, and beef stock and season to taste with salt and pepper. Pour over the veal in the casserole dish. Cover the dish tightly with foil.

5 **COOK** in the hot oven 1½ to 2 hours until the meat is tender and falling off the bone. Serve with a helping of the saffron risotto.

BROILED STEAK, FLORENTINE-STYLE, WITH STUFFED MUSHROOMS

TAGLIATA CON I FUNGHI

SERVES 4   PREPARATION TIME: 15 MINUTES   COOKING TIME: 20 MINUTES

Broiled steak is popular in Florence and is usually so large that it extends over the entire plate. This more elegant version matches the steak with a roasted mushroom, stuffed with a fragrant mix of fennel, garlic, tomato, cheese, and basil.

---

2 tablespoons **olive oil**, plus extra for greasing

8 large field **mushrooms**

1 small bulb **fennel**, finely chopped

8 tablespoons finely chopped **sun-dried tomatoes**

1 clove **garlic**, crushed

¼ pound freshly grated **fontina cheese**

¼ cup freshly grated **Parmesan cheese**

1 small handful fresh **basil leaves**, torn

salt and freshly ground **black pepper**

4 **sirloin steaks**, around ½ pound each, trimmed

extra-virgin olive oil, to serve

1 **GREASE** a baking sheet with a little olive oil. Remove the stems from the mushrooms and dice very finely with 4 of the caps, then set on one side. Arrange the 4 remaining mushroom caps, open side up, on the greased sheet and also set aside. Heat the oven to 350°F.

2 **HEAT** the remaining oil in a large sauté pan (see page 17) over a low heat. Add the fennel and cook 5 minutes until soft. Toss in the sun-dried tomatoes, garlic, and diced mushrooms and cook another 2 to 3 minutes. Remove from the pan and set aside to cool.

3 **BLEND** the grated cheeses and basil into the cooled mushroom mixture and season to taste with salt and pepper. Spoon equal amounts of the mixture over the 4 mushroom caps on the baking sheet.

4 **COOK** the stuffed mushrooms in the heated oven about 20 minutes until the mushrooms are tender.

5 **SEASON** the steaks well with salt and pepper. Heat a ribbed skillet or broiler until really hot and use to cook the steaks to your liking. Serve each with a roasted mushroom, drizzled with extra-virgin olive oil.

PORK FILLETS WITH WHITE WINE AND ROSEMARY

FILETTO DI MAIALE AL VINO BIANCO E ROSMARINO

SERVES 4   PREPARATION TIME: 20 MINUTES   COOKING TIME: 10 MINUTES

This is the perfect recipe for a quick supper. The rosemary in the sauce gives it a delicious uplifting freshness.

---

2 **pork** fillets, approximately 1 pound each, trimmed

½ cup **all-purpose flour**, seasoned with **salt** and freshly ground **black pepper**

1 stick **butter**

1 tablespoon **olive oil**

5 tablespoons dry **white wine**

½ cup **chicken stock** *(see page 18)*

1 handful fresh **rosemary**, chopped

1 **CUT** each pork fillet, slightly on the diagonal, into 6 thin slices, or escalopes. Dip these in the seasoned flour to coat them well.

2 **HEAT** half the butter with the oil in a large sauté pan (see page 17). Add half the pork escalopes and cook about 2 minutes on each side, until lightly browned. Remove from the pan and keep warm. Repeat with the remaining escalopes, then put aside with the first batch.

3 **ADD** the white wine, chicken stock, and fresh rosemary to the pan and allow to bubble up for 1 minute. Whisk in the remaining butter and season to taste with salt and pepper.

4 **RETURN** the pork to the pan and leave for 1 minute. Divide among 4 warm serving plates. Serve immediately.

LIVER WITH ONIONS
FEGATO ALLA VENEZIANA

SERVES 4   PREPARATION TIME: 15 MINUTES   COOKING TIME: 20 MINUTES

The sweetness of the onions contrasts brilliantly with the liver.

---

2 tablespoons **olive oil**

½ stick **butter**

2 large **onions**, very finely sliced

1 clove **garlic**, crushed

1 pound **calves' liver**, membranes removed and sliced thinly

1 large handful **flat-leaf parsley**, chopped

½ cup dry **white wine**

salt and freshly ground **black pepper**

1 recipe quantity **"wet" polenta** *(see page 27)*

1 **HEAT** the olive oil with the butter in a large sauté pan (see page 17). Add the onions and garlic. Stir to coat them well, then turn the heat down to very low and cook, stirring occasionally 10 to 15 minutes, until soft and golden.

2 **REMOVE** the onions and garlic from the pan and put on one side. Turn the heat up to high. Add the slices of liver and cook 1 to 2 minutes on each side until golden brown (the inside should remain pink). Return the onions to the pan with the parsley and white wine and cook a further 2 minutes.

3 **SEASON** to taste with salt and pepper and divide among 4 warm serving plates. Serve immediately, accompanied by the "wet" polenta.

LEG OF LAMB WITH HERB CRUST

COSCIOTTO D'AGNELLO IN CROSTA D'ERBE

SERVES 4 TO 6   PREPARATION TIME: 10 MINUTES
COOKING TIME: 1 TO 1½ HOURS, PLUS 15 MINUTES RESTING TIME

This recipe is fabulous for a casual lunch or dinner. The crunchy herb topping gives the lamb a really special touch.

4 to 4½ pounds leg of **lamb**

salt and freshly ground **black pepper**

6 tablespoons fresh **white breadcrumbs**

2 tablespoons freshly grated **Parmesan cheese**

2 cloves **garlic**, crushed

1 handful fresh **oregano**, finely chopped

1 handful fresh **rosemary**, finely chopped

1 handful **flat-leaf parsley**, finely chopped

3 tablespoons **olive oil**

1 cup **warm water**

1 **HEAT** the oven to 400°F. Place the lamb in a roasting pan and cut several slashes in the top of the meat using a sharp knife. Season well with salt and pepper.

2 **MIX** together the breadcrumbs, cheese, garlic, oregano, rosemary, parsley, and olive oil in a bowl to make a paste. Spread this mixture over the top of the lamb and rub it well into the cut surface. Pour the warm water into the base of the pan.

3 **ROAST** the lamb in the hot oven 15 minutes per pound for medium-rare meat, or 20 minutes for medium.

4 **REMOVE** the lamb from the oven and leave to rest in a warm place 15 minutes to allow the juices to settle. Slice and serve.

VEAL ESCALOPES WITH LEMON AND CAPERS

PICCATA DI VITELLO AL LIMONE E CAPPERI

SERVES 4 PREPARATION TIME: 10 MINUTES COOKING TIME: 15 MINUTES

The slight tanginess that the lemon brings to the sauce complements the veal beautifully.

4 **veal** escalopes (around ¼ pound each)

½ cup all-purpose **flour**, seasoned with **salt** and freshly ground **black pepper**

1 tablespoon **olive oil**

¼ stick **butter**

juice and grated zest of 1 **lemon**

¾ cup dry **white wine**

¾ cup **chicken** or **vegetable stock**
    (see page 18 or 19)

2 tablespoons **capers**, drained and rinsed

2 tablespoons **flat-leaf parsley**, chopped

1 **PLACE** the veal escalopes between 2 pieces of plastic wrap and beat with the rounded end of a rolling pin or the flat side of a meat mallet until really thin. Dip each piece of veal in the seasoned flour until lightly coated.

2 **HEAT** the oil and butter in a large sauté pan (see page 17). Add the veal and cook about 2 minutes on each side until lightly brown. Remove from the pan, put to one side, and keep warm.

3 **ADD** the lemon juice and zest, the white wine, and the chicken stock to the pan and bring to a boil. Allow to boil rapidly 3 to 4 minutes until about half the liquid has evaporated. Lower the heat.

4 **RETURN** the veal to the pan and coat well with the sauce, then stir in the capers and chopped parsley.

5 **SEASON** to taste with salt and pepper and serve immediately.

VEAL WITH TUNA SAUCE

VITELLO TONNATO

SERVES 4   PREPARATION TIME: 30 MINUTES
COOKING TIME: 1 HOUR, PLUS 2 HOURS COOLING TIME

This recipe makes a great addition to any summer menu. At first glance the mix of flavors may seem a little unusual, but they work together really well.

1¾ pounds boneless **veal** in a single piece

1¼ cups dry **white wine**

1 **onion**, quartered

1 small **carrot**, chopped

1 stalk **celery**, chopped

2 cloves **garlic**, chopped

2 **bay leaves**

3 **black peppercorns**

2 hard-boiled **egg yolks**

1 x 12 ounce can **tuna** in water, well drained

3 **anchovy** fillets, drained and rinsed

1 tablespoon **capers**, rinsed, plus extra to garnish

2 tablespoons **extra-virgin olive oil**

juice and grated zest of 1 **lemon**, plus slices to garnish

freshly ground **black pepper**

1 **PLACE** the veal in a large saucepan. Add the white wine, onion, carrot, celery, garlic, bay leaves, and peppercorns. Add just enough cold water to cover. Bring to a boil, turn down the heat, and leave to simmer gently 1 hour. Turn off the heat and leave the veal to cool in the liquid.

2 **COMBINE** the egg yolks, tuna, anchovies, and capers in a blender or food processor. With the motor running, slowly pour the olive oil in a thin stream into the blender or food processor until it is absorbed and the mixture is smooth. Transfer to a bowl, stir in the lemon juice and zest, and season to taste with pepper.

3 **REMOVE** the veal from the poaching liquid, slice thinly, and arrange on a serving platter. Strain the liquid and add just enough to the tuna sauce to give it the consistency of heavy cream.

4 **POUR** the tuna sauce over the sliced veal to coat it. Garnish with the extra capers and lemon slices and serve.

CHICKEN WITH WHITE WINE, TOMATOES, AND VEGETABLES *POLLO ALLA CACCIATORA*

SERVES 4   PREPARATION TIME: 35 MINUTES   COOKING TIME: 25 MINUTES

The aroma from this rustic chicken dish, as it bubbles away gently on the stove, is utterly irresistible.

4 **chicken** thighs and 4 drumsticks

4 tablespoons **olive oil**

1 large **onion**, sliced

1 **carrot**, finely diced

1 stalk **celery**, finely diced

6 ounces thickly sliced **pancetta**, finely diced

⅓ pound button **mushrooms**, sliced

2 cloves **garlic**, crushed

1 tablespoon **tomato paste**

3 cups canned **chopped tomatoes**

4 fresh **tomatoes**, peeled, deseeded, and chopped

½ cup dry **white wine**

3 sprigs fresh **oregano**

1 **bay leaf**

salt and freshly ground **black pepper**

1 PLACE the chicken in a large bowl and mix with 2 tablespoons of the olive oil until well coated. Heat a large, high-sided sauté pan (see page 17), add half the chicken, and cook over a medium-high heat about 7 to 10 minutes until lightly brown on all sides. Remove from the pan with a slotted spoon and put to one side. Repeat with the remaining chicken and set aside with the first batch.

2 WIPE out the pan with paper towels. Add the remaining oil and heat over a medium heat. Toss in the onion, carrot, and celery and cook 3 minutes, stirring often to prevent browning. Add the pancetta, mushrooms, and garlic and cook a further 2 minutes.

3 STIR in the tomato paste, canned tomatoes, fresh tomatoes, white wine, oregano, and the bay leaf, and season to taste with salt and pepper.

4 RETURN the chicken to the pan, lower the heat, and leave to simmer gently, covered, 25 minutes until the chicken is completely cooked through and the sauce has thickened slightly. Serve.

DEVILED CHICKEN

POLLO ALLA DIAVOLA

SERVES **4**   PREPARATION TIME: **35** MINUTES   COOKING TIME: **20** MINUTES

This recipe is traditionally prepared using poussins (small chickens), which are perfect for cooking under a domestic broiler. The amount of chili added to the marinade can be varied, according to how "hot" you like your food.

4 **poussins** (small chickens), around
   1¾ pounds each

8 tablespoons **olive oil**

juice and zest of 2 large **lemons**

2 small **red chilies**, deseeded and finely diced

2 cloves **garlic**, crushed

2 handfuls **flat-leaf parsley**, finely chopped

2 tablespoons **butter**, softened

lemon wedges, to serve

1 REMOVE the backbone from each poussin, using a pair of poultry shears or strong kitchen scissors, then flatten out. Pierce through with skewers if desired, to retain the shape. Place in a shallow casserole dish, large enough to hold all the birds in a single layer.

2 MIX together the olive oil, lemon juice and zest, diced chilies, and garlic in a small bowl and pour over the poussins. Leave in the fridge to marinate about 30 minutes.

3 HEAT the broiler to high. Place the poussins on a large broiler pan and cook under the hot broiler 5 to 7 minutes, basting occasionally with any remaining marinade until they are golden brown on top. Turn over and cook a further 5 to 7 minutes until golden brown on the other side. Lower the heat to medium and continue broiling the poussins until they are completely cooked. To test, pierce a thigh with a skewer—the juices should run clear, with no trace at all of any blood.

4 COMBINE the parsley and butter in a small bowl. As soon as the birds are cooked, transfer them to 4 warm plates, top with the parsley butter mixture, and serve, accompanied by the lemon wedges.

CHICKEN WITH TALEGGIO AND PROSCIUTTO

POLLO AL TALEGGIO E PROSCIUTTO

SERVES 4   PREPARATION TIME: 10 MINUTES   COOKING TIME: 20 MINUTES

Slice through these delicious morsels of tender chicken to reveal the fragrant basil and creamy, melted cheese in the center.

---

4 **chicken** breasts, about ½ pound each, skin removed

¼ pound **Taleggio cheese** *(see page 10)*, cut into small cubes

8 fresh **basil leaves**

freshly ground **black pepper**

8 slices **Parma ham** *(see page 13)*

2 tablespoons **olive oil**

1 **CUT** a small "pocket" in each chicken breast, taking care not to cut all the way through the meat. Stuff each "pocket" with a quarter of the Taleggio cheese, then press it firmly closed.

2 **PLACE** 2 basil leaves on top of each piece of chicken, season well with pepper, and wrap in the Parma ham, allowing 2 slices for each breast. The ham should be wrapped around the center of the chicken breast but not encase it completely. Brush each breast lightly with oil. Heat the oven to 400°F.

3 **HEAT** a large skillet over a medium heat. Add the prepared chicken and cook about 2 minutes on each side until lightly brown all over. Remove from the skillet and arrange in a single layer on a baking sheet.

4 **BAKE** the chicken in the hot oven 10 to 15 minutes until cooked through. Remove from the oven and leave to rest about 5 minutes before serving. Serve with oven-baked potatoes, if liked (see page 138).

CHARBROILED RED MULLET WITH OLIVES AND POTATOES

TRIGLIA GRIGLIATA CON OLIVE E PATATE

SERVES 4   PREPARATION TIME: 20 MINUTES   COOKING TIME: 10 MINUTES

The flavors are superbly matched in this simple, quick-to-prepare dish.

---

8 **red mullet** fillets, about ¼ pound each

2 tablespoons **olive oil**

1 small **red onion**, finely sliced

8 tablespoons pimento-stuffed **green olives**

juice and grated zest of 1 **lemon**

6 ounces marinated **artichoke hearts**, cut into small chunks

4 tablespoons **flat-leaf parsley**, roughly chopped

5 tablespoons **extra-virgin olive oil**

1 pound baby **new potatoes**, cut in half

freshly ground **black pepper**

lemon wedges, to serve

1 **BRUSH** the red mullet lightly with the olive oil and leave in the fridge while preparing the rest of the ingredients.

2 **MIX** together the red onion, green olives, lemon juice and zest, artichoke hearts, parsley, and 3 tablespoons of the extra-virgin olive oil in a large bowl and put to one side. Boil or steam the potatoes until tender. Add the warm potatoes to the onion, olive, and artichoke mixture, season to taste with pepper, and combine well. Put to one side and keep warm.

3 **HEAT** a ribbed skillet (see page 16) or large ordinary skillet until hot. Remove the fish from the fridge and place in the hot pan. Cook about 2 minutes on each side until cooked through.

4 **DIVIDE** the warm potato mixture among 4 warm serving plates. Top each serving with 2 of the freshly cooked fish fillets, drizzle over the remaining extra-virgin olive oil, and serve with the lemon wedges.

SEAFOOD WITH TOMATO

CACCIUCCO ALLA LIVORNESE

SERVES 4 PREPARATION TIME: 20 MINUTES COOKING TIME: 55 MINUTES

Traditionally this recipe was prepared using five different types of seafood—one for every "c" in the word "cacciucco."

3 tablespoons olive oil

1 onion, finely chopped

2 cloves garlic, crushed

1 carrot, diced

1 stalk celery, diced

2 tablespoons tomato paste

3 cups canned chopped tomatoes

½ cup dry white wine

2 cups fish stock (see page 19)

1 handful fresh dill, roughly chopped

1 pound monkfish fillets

12 fresh mussels

⅓ pound scallops

⅓ pound shrimp, shelled

salt and freshly ground black pepper

1 handful flat-leaf parsley, chopped

1 HEAT the oil in a large sauté pan (see page 17). Add the onion and cook 2 to 3 minutes until just soft. Add the garlic, carrot, and celery and cook another 3 minutes.

2 STIR in the tomato paste and cook 2 minutes, then add the chopped tomatoes, white wine, fish stock, and dill. Lower the heat, and leave to simmer gently 30 to 40 minutes until the vegetables are tender and the sauce has reduced by about one-third and thickened slightly.

3 CUT the monkfish into bite-size pieces. Clean the mussels thoroughly and remove the beards with a sharp knife. Discard any in shells that are broken or remain open when tapped.

4 ADD the monkfish to the hot tomato sauce and cook 5 minutes. Toss in the mussels, scallops, and shrimp and cook a further 4 minutes, or until all of the fish is cooked through.

5 SEASON to taste with salt and pepper, sprinkle over the chopped parsley, and serve immediately.

MARINATED SWORDFISH

PESCE SPADA MARINATO

SERVES 4   PREPARATION TIME: 35 MINUTES   COOKING TIME: 8 MINUTES

*The subtle addition of chili and lemon helps to lift the rich flavor
of the swordfish.*

4 **swordfish** steaks, about ½ pound each

juice and grated zest of 2 **lemons**

4 tablespoons **olive oil**

1 small **red chili**, deseeded and finely diced

1 clove **garlic**, crushed

½ cup dry **white wine**

freshly ground **black pepper**

extra-virgin olive oil, to serve

1 handful **flat-leaf parsley**, roughly chopped

1 ARRANGE the swordfish steaks in a shallow ovenproof dish, large enough to hold them in a single layer. Mix together the lemon juice and zest, olive oil, chili, garlic, and white wine in a small bowl and pour over the fish. Leave to marinate in the fridge 30 minutes.

2 HEAT a large skillet over a medium-high heat. Add the fish steaks, with any marinade, and cook about 3 minutes on each side until light brown and cooked through. Season to taste with pepper.

3 DIVIDE the fish steaks among 4 warm serving plates. Drizzle over a little extra-virgin olive oil, sprinkle with the chopped parsley, and serve.

SEA BASS WITH SALSA VERDE

BRANZINO CON SALSA VERDE

**SERVES 4   PREPARATION TIME: 15 MINUTES, PLUS 2 HOURS CHILLING TIME
COOKING TIME: 10 MINUTES**

The salsa verde is at its best when made a few hours in advance and kept in the fridge until needed. It goes as well with chicken as it does with fish.

½ cup fresh **white breadcrumbs**

1 tablespoon **milk**

2 **anchovy** fillets, rinsed

1 tablespoon **capers**, rinsed

1 large handful each **flat-leaf parsley**, **mint**, and **basil**, finely chopped

1 clove **garlic**, crushed

4 tablespoons **extra-virgin olive oil**

juice of ½ **lemon**

salt and freshly ground **black pepper**

8 **sea bass** fillets, about ¼ pound each

1 tablespoon **olive oil**

1 MIX together the breadcrumbs and milk in a bowl. Chop the anchovy fillets and capers together very finely and add to the breadcrumb mixture. Stir in the finely chopped herbs, garlic, extra-virgin olive oil, and lemon juice, then season to taste with salt and pepper. Leave this salsa verde mixture in the fridge at least 2 hours, preferably longer, before using.

2 TRIM the fish fillets, taking care to remove any remaining bones.

3 HEAT the tablespoon of olive oil in a large skillet. Add the sea bass fillets and cook about 2 minutes on each side until just cooked. Divide the fish among 4 warm plates and serve immediately, with a large spoonful of the salsa verde on top of each serving.

SOLE VENETIAN-STYLE

SOGLIOLA ALLA VENEZIANA

SERVES 4   PREPARATION TIME: 15 MINUTES   COOKING TIME: 15 MINUTES

The fresh herbs blend beautifully with the delicate flavor of the sole.

1¼ sticks **butter**

1 **onion**, diced

1 clove **garlic**, crushed

½ cup fresh **white breadcrumbs**

1 large handful **flat-leaf parsley**, chopped

1 large handful fresh **mint**, chopped

1 tablespoon **olive oil**

4 whole **sole**, approximately ¾ pound each, gutted and trimmed

salt and freshly ground **black pepper**

juice of 1 **lemon**

1 **MELT** the butter in a saucepan over a low heat. Add the onion and garlic and cook about 2 to 3 minutes, until the onion begins to soften.

2 **STIR** in the breadcrumbs, parsley, and mint and mix well. Put to one side to cool. Heat the oven to 350°F.

3 **OIL** a rimmed baking sheet, large enough to hold the fish in a single layer, with a splash of the olive oil. Arrange the fish on the tray, drizzle over the remaining oil, then spread the herbed breadcrumbs equally over the fish. Season to taste with with salt and pepper and drizzle over the lemon juice.

4 **BAKE** in the hot oven about 15 minutes until the fish is cooked through and the breadcrumbs are golden brown. Serve immediately.

BROILED TUNA WITH RED BELL PEPPER SAUCE *TONNO ALLA GRIGLIA CON PEPERONATA*

SERVES 4   PREPARATION TIME: 10 MINUTES   COOKING TIME: 25 MINUTES

The colors in the red pepper sauce are as spectacular as the taste.

4 **tuna** steaks, approximately ½ pound each

4 tablespoons **olive oil**

1 **onion**, chopped

1 **red chili**, deseeded and finely chopped

2 cloves **garlic**, crushed

3 **red bell peppers**, finely sliced

3 large ripe **tomatoes**, peeled, deseeded, and chopped

salt and freshly ground **black pepper**

1 BRUSH the tuna steaks lightly with a little of the olive oil and leave in the fridge while preparing the pepper sauce.

2 HEAT the remaining oil in a large sauté pan (see page 17), add the onion and cook 2 to 3 minutes, until soft. Add the chili and garlic and cook a further 1 minute. Stir in the bell peppers and tomatoes and leave to simmer 10 to 15 minutes until the bell peppers are soft and the sauce has thickened. Season to taste with salt and pepper, then set aside and keep warm.

3 HEAT a large ribbed skillet (see page 16) or ordinary skillet over a medium-high heat. Remove the tuna steaks from the fridge and place in the pan. Cook about 2 minutes on each side so that the tuna is brown on the outside but still slightly pink in the center.

4 TRANSFER the tuna steaks to 4 warm serving plates. Spoon over the red bell pepper sauce and serve immediately.

OVEN-BAKED POTATOES

PATATE AL FORNO

SERVES 4   PREPARATION TIME: 15 MINUTES   COOKING TIME: 50 MINUTES

The lemon gives these delicious golden potatoes a refreshing zing.

1¼ pounds **potatoes**, peeled and cut into approximately ½ inch cubes

3 cloves **garlic**, crushed

juice of 1 **lemon**

3 tablespoons **olive oil**

1 large handful fresh **rosemary**, roughly chopped

salt and freshly ground **black pepper**

1 **HEAT** the oven to 400°F.

2 **PLACE** all of the ingredients in a large bowl, seasoning well with salt and pepper, and toss to combine.

3 **SPREAD** over a large, lightly greased baking sheet and cook in the hot oven 45 to 50 minutes until the potatoes are golden brown and cooked through. Turn the potatoes 2 or 3 times during cooking, so that they brown evenly.

4 **TIP** the potatoes into a warm serving dish and serve.

EGGPLANT GRATIN

MELANZANE GRATINATE

SERVES 4   PREPARATION TIME: 20 MINUTES   COOKING TIME: 30 MINUTES

This gratin makes a delicious and satisfying supper dish and also makes a good accompaniment to simple meat and poultry dishes.

2 large **eggplants**, cut into cubes

3 **zucchinis**, cut into cubes

1 **onion**, diced

1 clove **garlic**, crushed

1 small handful fresh **thyme**, roughly chopped

4 tablespoons **olive oil**

salt and freshly ground **black pepper**

3 tablespoons freshly grated **Parmesan cheese**

8 tablespoons grated **mozzarella cheese**

1 **HEAT** the oven to 350°F. Place the cubes of the eggplants and zucchinis with the onion, garlic, and fresh thyme in an ovenproof casserole dish. Add the olive oil and stir to mix well. Season to taste with salt and pepper.

2 **COVER** the dish with foil or a well-fitting lid and cook in the hot oven 15 to 20 minutes until the vegetables are beginning to soften.

3 **UNCOVER** the dish and sprinkle the Parmesan and mozzarella cheeses over the top. Return to the oven a further 10 minutes until the vegetables are soft and the cheese topping is golden brown. Serve.

POTATO AND HERB GRATIN

PATATE GRATINATE ALLE ERBE AROMATICHE

SERVES 4   PREPARATION TIME: 20 MINUTES   COOKING TIME: 50 MINUTES

Make this for a Sunday lunch or a special dinner. It goes together perfectly with broiled and roasted meats, especially roast lamb.

1¾ pounds **potatoes**, thinly sliced

2 sprigs each fresh **thyme**, **sage**, and **rosemary**

2 cups **heavy cream**

1 stick **butter**

1 clove **garlic**, crushed

salt and freshly ground **black pepper**

4 tablespoons freshly grated **Parmesan cheese**

1 **HEAT** the oven to 400°F.

2 **LAYER** the potato slices in a large ovenproof dish.

3 **HEAT** the cream, butter, garlic, and herbs in a medium saucepan over a low heat until the mixture just begins to simmer. Remove from the heat and leave to stand 10 minutes for the flavors to infuse. Season to taste with salt and pepper.

4 **STRAIN** the cream mixture over the potatoes, discarding the herbs and garlic. Sprinkle over the Parmesan cheese and bake in the hot oven for 30 to 35 minutes until the potatoes are soft and the top is golden brown. Allow to cool slightly, then serve.

WARM CANNELLINI BEANS WITH TOMATOES AND HERBS *FAGIOLI ALL'UCCELLETTO*

**SERVES 4 PREPARATION TIME: 10 MINUTES, PLUS 8 HOURS SOAKING TIME
COOKING TIME: 1 TO 1½ HOURS**

The fresh herbs and splash of balsamic vinegar provide a touch of sharpness that contrasts well with the creaminess of the warm beans.

---

1 cup dried **cannellini beans**

1 **bay leaf**

3 sprigs fresh **rosemary**

3 sprigs fresh **thyme**

4 tablespoons **extra-virgin olive oil**

1 **red onion**, sliced

1 clove **garlic**, crushed

3 **tomatoes**, peeled, deseeded, and chopped

1 large handful **flat-leaf parsley**, chopped

1 large handful fresh **rosemary**, chopped

2 tablespoons **balsamic vinegar** *(see page 10)*

salt and freshly ground **black pepper**

1 **SOAK** the dried beans in a pan of cold water at least 8 hours, preferably overnight. Drain, place in a large clean saucepan, and cover with plenty of fresh cold water. Add the bay leaf, rosemary, and thyme and bring to a boil. Lower the heat and leave to simmer gently about 1 hour until the beans are just soft. Drain, rinse thoroughly in fresh cold water, and put to one side.

2 **HEAT** the oil in a large sauté pan (see page 17). Add the red onion and cook over a low heat about 3 minutes until soft. Add the garlic and cook a further 1 minute.

3 **STIR** in the tomatoes and cooked beans. Turn the heat up to medium and leave to simmer 5 minutes.

4 **MIX** in the chopped parsley and rosemary, then add the balsamic vinegar, and season to taste with salt and pepper. Remove from the heat and leave to cool slightly. Serve warm.

PEAS WITH PANCETTA AND MINT

PISELLI CON PANCETTA E MENTA

SERVES 4   PREPARATION TIME: 10 MINUTES   COOKING TIME: 25 MINUTES

With the tang of fresh green mint and the salty sharpness of the pinky-brown pancetta, this is a dish that looks and tastes fabulous.

1 pound shelled fresh **peas**

1 tablespoon **olive oil**

¼ pound thickly sliced **pancetta**, diced

1 handful fresh **mint**, finely chopped

¼ stick **butter**

freshly ground **black pepper**

1 **BRING** a large pan of salted water to a boil. Add the peas and return to a boil. Lower the heat slightly and leave to simmer about 15 minutes until the peas are tender. Drain and set aside.

2 **HEAT** the oil in a sauté pan (see page 17). Add the pancetta and cook about 3 to 4 minutes until just starting to brown.

3 **TOSS** in the cooked peas, followed by the chopped mint and butter, then season to taste with pepper. Remove from the heat, stir well to combine, and serve.

GARBANZO SALAD WITH TUNA

INSALATA DI CECI E TONNO

SERVES 4 PREPARATION TIME: 10 MINUTES, PLUS 30 MINUTES STANDING TIME

This quickly prepared salad is brimming with fresh flavors. Serve it for lunch with chunks of crusty bread or as a side dish at a dinner or party.

2 cups canned **garbanzos**, rinsed and drained

1 cup canned **tuna** in brine, rinsed, drained, and flaked

1 clove **garlic**, crushed

1 **red onion**, finely sliced

juice of 2 **lemons**

½ cup **extra-virgin olive oil**

freshly ground **black pepper**

2 handfuls **flat-leaf parsley**, chopped

1 handful **arugula**

1 **COMBINE** the garbanzos, tuna, garlic, and red onion in a large bowl and put to one side.

2 **WHISK** together the lemon juice and olive oil in a small bowl or cup and pour over the garbanzo mixture.

3 **SEASON** well with pepper, cover, and leave to stand in a cool place 30 minutes to allow the flavors to blend. Mix in the chopped parsley.

4 **PLACE** the arugula on a serving platter, spoon over the garbanzo and tuna mixture, and serve.

FRESH TOMATO SALAD WITH COUNTRY BREAD *PANZANELLA*

SERVES 4　PREPARATION TIME: 5 MINUTES, PLUS 30 MINUTES STANDING TIME

This stunning combination of chewy bread, fresh tomatoes, and tangy red-wine vinegar makes a refreshing addition to any summer meal.

½ pound loaf **ciabatta bread**, crusts removed and cut into small cubes

3 large fresh **tomatoes**, cut into small chunks

1 **yellow bell pepper**, cut into small chunks

½ **cucumber**, peeled and cut into small chunks

2 **scallions**, thinly sliced

1 small handful fresh **basil leaves**, torn

½ cup **extra-virgin olive oil**

3 tablespoons **red-wine vinegar**

1 clove **garlic**, crushed

1 **PLACE** the bread cubes with the chunks of tomato, yellow bell pepper, and cucumber in a large serving bowl. Add the scallions and basil and mix well together. Leave to stand in a cool place 30 minutes to allow the flavors to blend.

2 **WHISK** together the extra-virgin olive oil, red-wine vinegar, and garlic in a small bowl or cup. Pour over the bread, tomato, bell pepper, and cucumber salad mixture, toss to mix in, and serve immediately.

TOMATO, MINT, AND RED ONION SALAD

INSALATA DI POMODORO, MENTA E CIPOLLA

SERVES 4   PREPARATION TIME: 15 MINUTES

Mint serves as an uplifting and surprising contrast to the tangy tomato and crisp red onion in this salad.

---

4 large fresh **tomatoes**, finely sliced

½ small **red onion**, finely sliced

1 small handful fresh **mint**, chopped

3½ tablespoons **extra-virgin olive oil**

juice and grated zest of 1 **lemon**

freshly ground **black pepper**

1 **ARRANGE** the tomato slices on a serving plate, slightly overlapping. Sprinkle over the red onion and the mint.

2 **MIX** together the extra-virgin olive oil and the lemon juice and zest in a small bowl or cup and drizzle over the tomato and onion salad.

3 **SEASON** to taste with pepper and serve immediately.

FRESH MOZZARELLA AND TOMATO SALAD

INSALATA CAPRESE

SERVES 4   PREPARATION TIME: 15 MINUTES

The key to the success of this simple dish lies in the freshness and quality of the ingredients. Use only the very best available.

1 pound **buffalo mozzarella**

3 large, ripe, fresh **tomatoes**

1 small handful fresh **basil leaves**

salt and freshly ground **black pepper**

4 tablespoons **extra-virgin olive oil**

2 tablespoons **white-wine vinegar**

1 tablespoon **capers**, rinsed

1 SLICE the mozzarella and tomatoes thinly and arrange on a serving platter. Scatter over the basil leaves and season to taste with salt and a generous grinding of black pepper.

2 WHISK together the extra-virgin olive oil and white-wine vinegar in a small bowl or cup, then drizzle over the tomatoes and mozzarella. Scatter the capers over the top and serve.

ORANGE AND FENNEL SALAD

INSALATA SICILIANA

SERVES 4   PREPARATION TIME: 15 MINUTES

You can make this tangy salad in advance, if you like, but it is best to add the pine nuts just before serving.

---

4 large **oranges**, peeled and segmented

1 bulb **fennel**, trimmed and finely sliced

1 small handful fresh **dill**, chopped

3 tablespoons **extra-virgin olive oil**

1 tablespoon **white-wine vinegar**

3 tablespoons **pine nuts**, toasted

1 **PLACE** the oranges, fennel, and dill in a large serving bowl.

2 **POUR** over the olive oil and white-wine vinegar and toss well to combine. Set aside in a cool place, if you wish, until ready to serve.

3 **SPRINKLE** over the pine nuts and serve immediately.

POTATO SALAD WITH CAPERS

INSALATA DI PATATE CON CAPPERI

SERVES 4 PREPARATION TIME: 10 MINUTES, PLUS 30 MINUTES STANDING TIME
COOKING TIME: 15 MINUTES

Light and fresh, yet satisfying, this will become a warm-weather staple.

1½ pounds baby **new potatoes**

2 tablespoons **capers**, rinsed

3 **scallions**, finely chopped

2 tablespoons **red-wine vinegar**

3½ tablespoons **extra-virgin olive oil**

freshly ground **black pepper**

1 BOIL or steam the potatoes in their skins until tender, then set aside to cool. Cut any larger potatoes in quarters or halves, but leave the small ones whole.

2 MIX together all of the ingredients, including the prepared potatoes, in a large serving bowl, seasoning well with pepper.

3 LEAVE to stand at least 30 minutes before serving to allow the flavors to mix together.

ASPARAGUS SALAD

INSALATA DI ASPARAGI

SERVES 4   PREPARATION TIME: 20 MINUTES   COOKING TIME: 4 TO 6 MINUTES

This sumptuous mix of jewel-like cherry tomatoes and spears of fresh green asparagus creates a feast for the eyes as well as the palate.

1½ pounds fresh **asparagus**, trimmed

¼ pound **cherry tomatoes**, halved

1 small handful fresh **basil leaves**, torn

3 tablespoons **extra-virgin olive oil**

1 tablespoon **balsamic vinegar** *(see page 10)*

salt and freshly ground **black pepper**

1 **STEAM** the asparagus 4 to 6 minutes until just tender. Cool immediately under cold running water, pat dry, and arrange on a serving platter.

2 **MIX** together the cherry tomatoes and basil in a bowl and set aside.

3 **WHISK** together the extra-virgin olive oil and balsamic vinegar in another bowl or cup and season to taste with salt and pepper. Pour over the tomatoes and basil and toss to mix in well.

4 **TIP** the tomato mixture over the platter of asparagus and serve.

ITALIAN CREAMS

PANNA COTTA

SERVES 4 PREPARATION TIME: 20 MINUTES, PLUS 4 HOURS CHILLING TIME

The Italian name of this traditional dessert translates as "cooked cream."
It is very simple to make and tastes delicious served with fresh fruit.

2 sheets **leaf gelatin** *(see page 11)*

¾ cup **heavy cream**

¾ cup **milk**

2 tablespoons **superfine sugar**

1 teaspoon **vanilla extract**

fresh **fruit** in season, to serve

powdered sugar, to serve (optional)

1 PLACE the sheets of gelatin in a large bowl and cover completely with cold water. Leave 5 minutes until the gelatin has softened.

2 COMBINE the cream, milk, superfine sugar and vanilla extract in a small saucepan. Place over a low heat until just warm. Remove from the heat and put to one side.

3 REMOVE the gelatin from the water and squeeze out any excess moisture. Stir into the warm milk mixture until it dissolves. Leave to cool about 5 to 10 minutes.

4 DIVIDE the mixture equally among 4 small ramekins and place in the fridge to chill and set for at least 4 hours, preferably overnight. Carefully turn out of the ramekins, dust with powdered sugar (optional), and serve with a mixture of seasonal fresh fruit.

ZABAGLIONE

SERVES 4 PREPARATION TIME: 5 MINUTES COOKING TIME: 7 MINUTES

Marsala is a fortified wine that originates in Sicily. It is traditionally used in this luscious, rich, and creamy dessert—the perfect ending to any really special meal.

8 **egg yolks**

4 tablespoons **superfine sugar**

½ cup **Marsala wine** *(see page 12)*

8 **ladyfingers**

1 **WHISK** together the yolks, sugar, and Marsala in a heatproof bowl.

2 **PLACE** the bowl over a pan of gently simmering water, so that the base of the pan does not touch the water, and continue to whisk vigorously until the mixture is frothy and is just starting to thicken. This should take about 5 to 7 minutes. Remove the bowl from the heat.

3 **POUR** the warm egg and Marsala mixture into tall serving glasses and serve immediately, accompanied by the ladyfingers.

STRAWBERRIES IN BALSAMIC VINEGAR

FRAGOLE CON ACETO BALSAMICO

SERVES 4 PREPARATION TIME: 10 MINUTES

The addition of the balsamic vinegar may seem odd, but it really does help to bring out the full flavor of the fresh strawberries.

¾ pound fresh **strawberries**

1 tablespoon **superfine sugar**

1 tablespoon **balsamic vinegar** *(see page 10)*

4 scoops **vanilla ice cream**, to serve

1 WASH and hull the strawberries, cut in half, and place in a bowl.

2 SPRINKLE over the sugar and balsamic vinegar and toss well to combine.

3 PLACE a scoop of ice cream on each serving dish and spoon over the strawberries. Serve immediately.

"PICK-ME-UP" PUDDING

TIRAMISÙ

SERVES 4 TO 6

PREPARATION TIME: 20 MINUTES, PLUS 2 HOURS CHILLING TIME

This sensational combination of fresh coffee, Marsala wine, and rich, creamy mascarpone cheese is utterly irresistible.

---

5 **egg yolks**

½ cup superfine **sugar**

½ pound **mascarpone cheese** *(see page 10)*

2 **egg whites**

1½ cups **espresso** or strong **coffee**, cold

4 tablespoons **Marsala wine**

20 **ladyfingers**

2 tablespoons **cocoa powder**

4 tablespoons grated **bittersweet chocolate**

1 WHISK the egg yolks and sugar together in a large bowl, preferably using an electric hand-held whisk, until thick and light in color. Add the mascarpone and combine well. Put to one side.

2 BEAT the egg whites in a clean bowl until they form stiff peaks, then carefully fold in the mascarpone mixture, using a large metal spoon. Put to one side.

3 MIX together the cold coffee and Marsala wine in another bowl. Dip half the ladyfingers into the mixture, being sure to soak them well, and use to line the base of a serving dish, approximately 11 inches x 7 inches. Pour over half of the prepared mascarpone mixture.

4 REPEAT with the remaining ladyfingers and mascarpone mixture.

5 SPRINKLE the cocoa powder over the top using a strainer, then scatter with the grated chocolate. Refrigerate for at least 2 hours, preferably overnight. Serve.

BAKED PEACHES STUFFED WITH AMARETTI COOKIES

PESCHE RIPIENE

SERVES 4 PREPARATION TIME: 10 MINUTES COOKING TIME: 15 TO 20 MINUTES

These delicious peaches, served warm with their amaretti filling, create a spectacular fusion of color and flavor.

4 ripe yellow **peaches**

¼ pound **amaretti cookies**, crushed

½ stick **butter**, melted

1 large **egg yolk**

1 teaspoon freshly grated **nutmeg**

whipped **cream**, to serve

1 **HEAT** the oven to 400°F.

2 **BRUSH** an ovenproof dish, large enough to contain the stuffed peaches in a single layer, with a little of the melted butter.

3 **CRUSH** the amaretti cookies in a food processor or blender, then mix in the remaining melted butter, egg yolk, and nutmeg.

4 **HALVE** the peaches and remove the pits. Spoon the prepared amaretti filling into each peach cavity and press down firmly. Arrange the stuffed peaches in the prepared ovenproof dish.

5 **BAKE** in the hot oven 15 to 20 minutes until soft and light brown. Serve warm with whipped fresh cream.

ICE CREAM WITH ESPRESSO AND FRANGELICO *AFFOGATO AL CAFFÈ*

SERVES 4   PREPARATION TIME: 5 MINUTES

Frangelico is a sweet, hazelnut liqueur from the Liguria region of Italy.
It is particularly good with the hot and cold taste sensations of this dessert.

---

8 scoops **vanilla ice cream**

4 tablespoons **espresso coffee**, hot

4 tablespoons **Frangelico** liqueur

1 PLACE 2 scoops of ice cream into each of 4 tall serving glasses. Put aside in the freezer until ready to serve.

2 POUR 1 tablespoon of hot espresso coffee and 1 tablespoon of Frangelico liqueur over each glass of ice cream and serve immediately.

LEMON ICE CREAM

GELATO AL LIMONE

SERVES 4   PREPARATION TIME: 20 MINUTES, PLUS FREEZING TIME

Creamy and luscious, this ice cream makes a glorious finale to a meal.

¾ cup **milk**

4 **egg yolks**

1 cup **superfine sugar**

juice and grated zest of 2 **lemons**

¾ cup **heavy cream**

1 HEAT the milk in a saucepan, over a low heat, until just warm. Put on one side.

2 WHISK together the egg yolks and sugar in a large bowl, then pour in the warm milk, whisking constantly. Return the mixture to the saucepan and stir over a low heat, with a wooden spoon, until the mixture is just thick enough to coat the back of the spoon. Do not allow to boil. Pour into a clean bowl and leave to cool completely.

3 STIR the lemon juice and zest into the cooled mixture, followed by the heavy cream. Pour into an ice-cream maker and freeze according to the manufacturer's instructions. Serve.

COFFEE ICE CREAM

GELATO AL CAFFÈ

SERVES 4 TO 6 PREPARATION TIME: 20 MINUTES, PLUS FREEZING TIME

Use the best quality coffee for the richest, smoothest flavor.

¾ cup **milk**

1 **vanilla bean**, split

2 **eggs**

⅔ cup **superfine sugar**

⅔ cup **espresso coffee**, cold

¾ cup **heavy cream**

1 HEAT the milk in a saucepan, with the vanilla bean, over a low heat, until just warm. Leave to stand 5 minutes, then remove the vanilla bean. Scrape out the vanilla seeds with a knife and add them to the milk, discarding the empty pod.

2 WHISK together the eggs and sugar in a large bowl, then pour in the warm milk, whisking constantly. Return the mixture to the saucepan and cook, over a low heat, stirring constantly with a wooden spoon until the mixture is just thick enough to coat the back of the spoon. Do not allow to boil.

3 POUR into a clean bowl and stir in the espresso coffee. Leave to cool completely.

4 STIR in the cream, then transfer to an ice-cream maker and freeze according to the manufacturer's instructions. Serve.

LEMON RICOTTA CAKE

TORTA DI RICOTTA AL LIMONE

SERVES 6 TO 8   PREPARATION TIME: 30 MINUTES   COOKING TIME: 45 MINUTES

This is a cross between a pudding and a cake. When served warm, the luscious creamy center is beautifully balanced by the tang of the lemon.

---

1 tablespoon melted **butter**

6 ounces ground **almonds**

2 ounces **plain flour**

5½ ounces **butter**, softened

7 ounces **superfine sugar**

4 **eggs**, separated

7 ounces **ricotta cheese**

juice and grated zest of 3 **lemons**

powdered sugar, to serve

1 **HEAT** the oven to 325°F. Grease an 8 inch springform cake pan with the melted butter. Line the base with baking parchment paper.

2 **MIX** together the almonds and flour in a bowl and put to one side.

3 **BEAT** the butter and sugar together until light and creamy. Add the egg yolks and continue beating until well combined. Mix in the ricotta cheese, followed by the lemon juice and zest. Fold in the almond and flour mixture until just combined. Put to one side.

4 **BEAT** the egg whites in a clean bowl until they just start to form stiff peaks, then gently fold into the cake mixture, using a metal spoon.

5 **POUR** into the prepared cake pan, smooth over the top, and bake in the hot oven about 45 minutes until lightly brown and still slightly soft in the center. Allow to cool slightly in the pan, then turn out. Serve warm or at room temperature, dusted with powdered sugar.

CHOCOLATE ICE-CREAM SLICE

SEMIFREDDO AL CIOCCOLATO

SERVES 6   PREPARATION TIME: 20 MINUTES, PLUS 4 HOURS FREEZING TIME

This ice-cream style of dessert does not require any churning, so can be frozen by simply popping it into the freezer. It has a rich and powerful chocolate flavor.

2 cups **heavy cream**

4 **eggs**, separated

1⅔ cups **superfine sugar**

¾ cup **cocoa powder**

2 tablespoons **Frangelico** liqueur *(see page 173)*

4 tablespoons toasted, chopped **hazelnuts**

fresh **raspberries**, to serve

1 MIX half the heavy cream with the egg yolks, superfine sugar, and cocoa powder in a saucepan until well combined. Place over a low heat and stir constantly until the mixture thickens and is just starting to boil. Remove from the heat, stir in the Frangelico liqueur, and transfer to a large bowl. Leave to cool completely.

2 LINE the base of an 8 inch springform cake pan with plastic wrap.

3 WHIP the remaining cream until thick in a clean bowl, then fold into the cold custard mixture. Beat the egg whites until they just start to form stiff peaks, then fold in the cream and custard mixture, using a metal spoon. Pour into the prepared cake pan and cover with plastic wrap to seal completely. Freeze at least 4 hours, preferably overnight.

4 REMOVE from the freezer and place in the fridge about 20 minutes before serving to soften slightly. Cut into slices and serve, sprinkled with the hazelnuts and a helping of fresh raspberries.

PANFORTE

**MAKES ABOUT 24 SLICES   PREPARATION TIME: 25 MINUTES
COOKING TIME: 15 MINUTES, PLUS OVERNIGHT COOLING TIME**

This traditional treat from Siena is perfect for rounding off a celebratory dinner in style, especially when served with a glass of chilled vin santo.

---

6 ounces each **hazelnuts**, **almonds**, and **walnuts**, roasted and roughly chopped

6 ounces each dried **figs**, dried **apricots**, and dried **prunes**, roughly chopped

1¼ cups **all-purpose flour**

pinch of **white pepper**

1 teaspoon grated **nutmeg**

½ teaspoon ground **cloves**

½ teaspoon ground **cilantro**

½ teaspoon ground **cinnamon**

⅔ cup **superfine sugar**

⅔ cup **honey**

powdered sugar, to serve

1 **LINE** a 10 inch springform cake pan with baking parchment paper. Put to one side. Heat the oven to 350°F.

2 **COMBINE** the chopped nuts and dried fruit in a large bowl. Add the flour, pepper, nutmeg, cloves, cilantro, and cinnamon and mix in thoroughly. Put to one side side.

3 **PLACE** the sugar and honey in a saucepan and bring to a boil over a low heat, stirring constantly. Allow to boil 1 minute, then remove from the heat and pour over the fruit and nut mixture, stirring to combine thoroughly. The mixture should be very thick.

4 **SPOON** into the prepared cake tin and smooth out evenly with slightly wet hands. Bake in the hot oven 15 minutes. Remove from the oven and leave to cool a little. While still warm, run a sharp knife around the edge to release it from the pan. Leave in the pan to cool completely overnight.

5 **REMOVE** from the pan and cut into thin slices. Dust lightly with powdered sugar just before serving.

WHITE PEACHES WITH RASPBERRIES, MINT, AND PROSECCO

PESCE BIANCHE CON LAMPONI, MENTA E PROSECCO

SERVES 4   PREPARATION TIME: 15 MINUTES   COOKING TIME: 5 MINUTES

Prosecco is an Italian white wine, made in the Champagne style, that is light and deliciously fragrant. The combination of luscious white peaches and raspberries, mixed with mint and Prosecco, is simply heaven on Earth and just perfect for a warm summer's evening.

⅔ cup **superfine sugar**

⅔ cup cold **water**

4 **white peaches**

½ pound **raspberries**

1 small handful fresh **mint**, finely shredded

⅔ cup dry **Prosecco**, chilled

1 **PLACE** the sugar and water in a saucepan over a low heat. Stir continuously until the sugar has dissolved completely. Remove from the heat and leave to cool, then set aside in the fridge to chill.

2 **SLICE** the peaches into a large bowl, then add the raspberries and mint. This should be done no more than 30 minutes before serving—any longer and the peaches will start to brown.

3 **MIX** together the chilled sugar syrup and Prosecco in a clean cup or bowl and pour over the peaches.

4 **SPOON** into 4 serving dishes and serve.

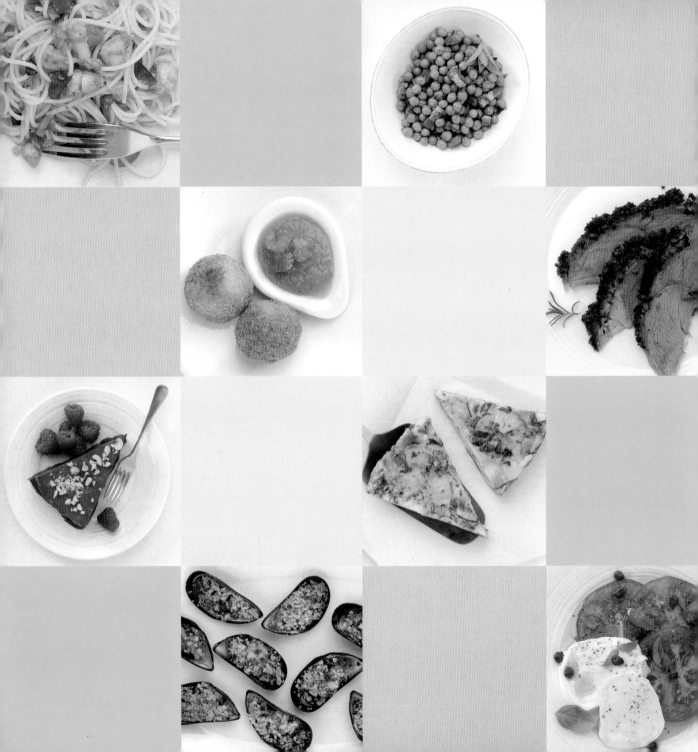

PART 3

THE MENUS

*Putting together a **successful** menu is one of the most challenging aspects of **entertaining** and can be a juggling act for even the most accomplished cook. Each of the **suggestions** that follows has been developed with a specific occasion in mind and is organized so that not only are the **flavors**, textures, and colors in the various dishes **balanced**, but the amount of preparation and last-minute **touches** that are required are too.*

*Each menu comes with a detailed time plan, **clearly** explaining exactly when to execute the various stages of the recipes involved. Preparation **notes** giving details of useful **techniques** are also included to make life as easy as possible.*

*While each of the menus has been designed with a particular **occasion** in mind, you should feel **free** to mix and match recipes to suit your own needs. Refer to the time plans for **guidance**, but do not feel constrained by any of the suggestions. Your cooking should reflect who you are and your **lifestyle** and most importantly be a source of **pleasure** to all who gather around your table.*

SIMPLE LUNCH

TIME PLAN

This is a truly simple lunch to prepare, offering a fabulous mix of contrasting flavors, textures, and colors. The sharp saltiness of the crunchy crostini helps to highlight the delicate taste of the asparagus that follows. Rounded off with a satisfying helping of fresh seafood pasta, this is a beautifully balanced meal.

CROSTINI WITH GARLIC, TOMATO, AND ANCHOVY

(see page 41)

ASPARAGUS WITH BALSAMIC VINEGAR AND PARMESAN

(see page 46)

SPAGHETTI WITH SHRIMP

(see page 73)

The day before, make crostini bases and store in an airtight tin. Prepare individual ingredients for the crostini topping, but do not mix together. Trim the asparagus and shave the Parmesan cheese. Clean and peel the shrimp. Place the topping ingredients, asparagus, Parmesan, and shrimp in covered containers in the fridge. Remember to halve the quantities of ingredients asked for in the recipes when serving just two people.

PM
12:30 ASSEMBLE the crostini. Preheat the oven for the asparagus.
1:00 SERVE the crostini. Place the asparagus in the oven.
1:20 PUT the water for the pasta on to boil and serve the asparagus.
1:35 COOK the pasta and prepare the sauce (while the pasta is cooking).
1:45 DRAIN the pasta, combine with the sauce, and serve.

PREPARATION NOTES

Buy the freshest **SHRIMP** you can find, still in the shell. They should be **RAW** shrimp rather than the precooked variety, as they will give a superior flavor and texture to the pasta dish. When you have **PEELED** them, run a sharp knife down the back of the shrimp and **WASH** away any gritty black residue that may have collected there.

LUNCH BOX

ZUCCHINI FRITTATA

(see page 50)

TOMATO, MINT, AND RED ONION SALAD

(see page 153)

ORANGE AND FENNEL SALAD

(see page 157)

PANFORTE

(see page 182)

TIME PLAN

This nourishing lunch is a good match of creamy, rich frittata with two tangy and unusual salads that will retain their freshness even on a hot day. It takes only a few moments to assemble and pack.

The panforte can be made up to three weeks in advance and stored in an airtight tin. The night before, prepare and combine all the salad ingredients, but do not add the dressings. Store them in sealed containers in the fridge. Prepare and keep the dressings in separate containers, also refrigerated. Make the frittata and keep, well covered, in the fridge. Note that the recipes used serve four and that quantities of ingredients should be adjusted to suit your own requirements.

In the morning, slice and pack the frittata. Pack the containers of salad and their dressings separately. Wrap and pack slices of panforte.

PM
12:45

1:00

POUR the dressings over the salads and mix well to combine.
SERVE the slices of frittata with the dressed salads. Round off lunch with the panforte.

PREPARATION NOTES

FENNEL is a delicious addition to many dishes and is used **WIDELY** throughout Italy. Buy only fresh unblemished bulbs. If you try to simply **REMOVE** and discard any bruised parts, you will find you have very little left, because the layers are very thick and you will lose most of the fennel. To prepare, remove the feathery **FRONDS** from the top of the fennel with a sharp knife and cut in half. Remove the central core and then **SLICE**. The fronds can be chopped up and used as a flavoring. Sprinkle any cut fennel with a little **LEMON** juice; otherwise it will turn brown very quickly.

MIDWEEK LUNCH WITH FAMILY

TIME PLAN

Clear, fresh flavors are the central theme of this quick and easy to prepare lunch menu. The tangy tomato soup offers a refreshing lead into the subtle seasoning of the chicken and asparagus, while the strawberries in balsamic vinegar make for a rich yet light finish in which the true taste of the fruit really shines through.

CREAMY TOMATO SOUP
(see page 70)

DEVILED CHICKEN
(see page 122)

ASPARAGUS SALAD
(see page 161)

STRAWBERRIES IN BALSAMIC VINEGAR
(see page 166)

The night before, make the soup and prepare all of the ingredients for the deviled chicken, but do not marinate. Trim and blanch the asparagus for the salad and cut up the cherry tomatoes. Make up the salad dressing. Store all the prepared food, except the asparagus, covered, in the fridge. Only chill the asparagus in very hot weather.

12:30 PM MARINATE the chicken, cover, and set aside in a cool place. Combine the salad ingredients in a serving bowl, but do not dress. Leave, covered, in a cool place.

1:00 HEAT the soup and serve. Heat the broiler.

1:15 COOK the chicken under the hot broiler until the juices run clear. Dress the salad and serve with the cooked chicken.

1:45 SPRINKLE the balsamic vinegar over the strawberries and serve.

PREPARATION NOTES

The easiest way to prepare ASPARAGUS is to simply bend the ends of the stems with your hand—the asparagus spear will always break at the point where it starts to become TENDER, leaving the woody part behind to be discarded. PEEL the remaining part of the stem with a vegetable peeler until it is the same thickness as the tip. This allows whole asparagus spears (tips and stems) to COOK evenly. Asparagus is a very tender vegetable, so take care not to overcook it.

MIDWEEK LUNCH WITH FRIENDS

TIME PLAN

MUSHROOM RISOTTO
(see page 98)

SOLE VENETIAN-STYLE
(see page 134)

FRESH TOMATO SALAD WITH COUNTRY BREAD
(see page 151)

BAKED PEACHES STUFFED WITH AMARETTI COOKIES
(see page 170)

All of the dishes, apart from the risotto, can be prepared almost completely in advance. The creamy, full-flavored risotto contrasts well with the delicate fish and the juicy salad. The richness of the amaretti biscuits blends beautifully with the sweet honeyed tang of the peaches.

The night before, slice the mushrooms and make the stock for the risotto (or defrost from the freezer). Halve and pit the peaches and stuff with the amaretti mixture. Cover and store in the fridge.

11:30 AM CHOP the ingredients for the fresh tomato salad. Combine everything, except the diced bread, in a large serving bowl. Cover and set aside in a cool place. Prepare the ingredients for the sole, again keeping them covered in a cool place.

12:00 PM DICE and cook the onions for the risotto. Turn off the heat and leave in the pan. Prepare the remaining risotto ingredients and put aside.

12:30 MAKE the risotto according to the recipe.

1:00 ADD the bread to the salad and prepare the dressing. Put both on one side, but do not combine. Serve the risotto.

1:20 COOK the sole and serve. Combine the salad and dressing and serve.

1:45 HEAT the oven for the peaches.

2:00 BAKE the stuffed peaches in the hot oven.

2:30 SERVE the peaches, with cream passed around separately.

PREPARATION NOTES

LEMON SOLE is a delicious flat fish that is very thin and will cook through quite quickly. Freshly made **WHITE** breadcrumbs are essential for coating the **FISH** when it is cooked Venetian-style. To make them, simply take a loaf of stale white bread and slice up roughly. Remove the crusts, then drop chunks through the feeding tube into a food processor, while the motor is running. Any breadcrumbs not used for coating the sole will keep well in the **FREEZER** for later use.

WEEKEND LUNCH WITH FAMILY

TIME PLAN

The soup is quite substantial, so just a small amount topped with a dash of extra-virgin olive oil will make an ideal start to this family lunch. The charbroiled steak is simpler and quicker to prepare than a full roast, and the lemon ricotta cake provides a luscious yet zesty ending.

PASTA AND BEAN SOUP

(see page 69)

BROILED STEAK, FLORENTINE-STYLE, WITH STUFFED MUSHROOMS

(see page 109)

PEAS WITH PANCETTA AND MINT

(see page 146)

LEMON RICOTTA CAKE

(see page 178)

The day or evening before, make the soup. Prepare and stuff the mushrooms and shell the peas. Keep everything, well covered, in the fridge until ready to use. Make the cake and store in a cool place.

PM 12:30 **HEAT** the oven for the mushrooms. Put the water for the peas on to boil. Warm the soup and serve.

1:00 **PLACE** the stuffed mushrooms in the hot oven. Cook the peas in the boiling water, then drain, and keep warm. Brown the pancetta and keep warm.

1:15 **COOK** the steaks to your preference. Finish off the peas and pancetta and serve with the steak and cooked mushrooms.

1:45 **SERVE** the cake (warm gently in a low oven about 10 minutes, if preferred), accompanied by cream and fresh raspberries if you wish.

PREPARATION NOTES

The lemon **RICOTTA** cake in this menu is guaranteed to become a firm family **FAVORITE**. It is particularly good served warm. One of the best ways to **WARM** it through is to cut it into serving **SLICES** first. Then place these in the microwave for about 30 seconds on a **MEDIUM** heat, just before serving.

WEEKEND LUNCH WITH FRIENDS

TIME PLAN

THICK VEGETABLE SOUP WITH PESTO

(see page 61)

CHICKEN WITH WHITE WINE, TOMATOES, AND VEGETABLES

(see page 121)

POTATO SALAD WITH CAPERS

(see page 158)

LEMON OR COFFEE ICE CREAM

(see page 174 or 177)

This menu is designed for maximum impact with minimum effort. The soup is fairly hearty, so do not be tempted to serve too much—make sure you leave your guests room for the dishes that follow. Ice cream is the ideal way to round off such a comforting meal.

Make the ice cream up to two days in advance and store in the freezer. The night before, make the soup and cook the potatoes for the salad. Prepare the other salad ingredients but do not combine with the potatoes. Keep everything, covered, in the fridge.

In the morning, make the chicken casserole and leave to cool on the stove. If it is a very hot day, keep in the fridge until required.

PM
1:00 **WARM** the soup over a low heat and serve.
1:30 **MIX** together all the ingredients for the potato salad and put to one side. Heat the chicken casserole until it is piping hot. Transfer to a serving dish, garnish, and take to the table. Serve the chicken and let your guests help themselves to the salad.
2:15 **TAKE** the ice cream out of the freezer and place in the refrigerator to soften for about 20 minutes.
2:35 **SERVE** the ice cream.

PREPARATION NOTES

When cooking the **POTATOES** for the salad, you will get the best **TEXTURE** if they are boiled or steamed whole. The easiest way to check if potatoes are cooked through enough, is to pierce them with a **SKEWER**—if the potato falls off the end easily they are **COOKED**; if not, leave them a few minutes more and then test again.

SIMPLE DINNER

Almost everything can be prepared well in advance for this easy dinner. The flavors are simple and direct, perfect for a truly relaxing, informal occasion. The chocolate ice-cream slice is very rich, however, so is best balanced with some fresh, juicy berries.

ANCHOVY AND GARLIC DIP

(see page 53)

FRESH MOZZARELLA AND TOMATO SALAD

(see page 154)

BRAISED BEEF WITH RED WINE, TUSCAN-STYLE

(see page 102)

CHOCOLATE ICE CREAM SLICE

(see page 181)

The day before, prepare the beef casserole and the chocolate ice cream slice. Make the vegetable crudités for the dip, cover with plastic wrap to prevent them drying out, and keep refrigerated. If you are serving this menu to two people, remember to halve the quantities of ingredients asked for in the recipes.

PM

7:30 PREPARE the dip and serve warm with the vegetable crudités.

8:00 WARM the beef casserole over a low heat, stirring from time to time. Prepare the mozzarella and tomato salad and serve.

8:30 SERVE the beef, with a helping of "wet" polenta (see page 27), if you wish.

9:00 REMOVE the chocolate ice-cream slice from the freezer and place in the refrigerator 20 minutes to soften slightly.

9:20 SERVE the chocolate ice-cream slice with fresh berries.

PREPARATION NOTES

When you are making the ice cream slice, be CAREFUL not to overwhip the cream. It should be just THICK enough to hold its SHAPE, but not stiff. If it is whipped too much, it will be difficult to FOLD into the mixture and you will end up with LUMPS of frozen cream that will SPOIL the smooth richness of the finished dish.

ROMANTIC DINNER

TIME PLAN

RISOTTO WITH SHRIMP AND CHAMPAGNE

(see page 101)

VEAL ESCALOPES WITH LEMON AND CAPERS

(see page 117)

OVEN-BAKED POTATOES

(see page 138)

ZABAGLIONE

(see page 165)

What could be better for a romantic dinner than a combination of Champagne, succulent, tender veal, and warm, melt-in-the-mouth zabaglione? This menu takes a little effort, but the results are truly sensational.

In the morning, collect and measure out all the ingredients (to serve two, halve all the recipe quantities given). Peel the shrimp and keep refrigerated. Chop the onion for the risotto and the capers and parsley for the veal. Cover and put aside in a cool place. Separate the eggs for the zabaglione and keep refrigerated, covered with plastic wrap.

PM
6:30 PEEL the potatoes, then chop up, and coat in the remaining ingredients.

7:00 HEAT the oven for the potatoes.

7:30 PLACE the potatoes in the hot oven. Prepare the risotto (and drink any left-over Champagne!).

7:50 TURN over the potatoes and serve the risotto.

8:15 COOK the veal and serve with the potatoes.

9:00 PREPARE the zabaglione and serve immediately with the ladyfingers.

PREPARATION NOTES

It is important to use really **THIN** pieces of veal for preparing the escalopes, so that they cook quickly. If you have **TROUBLE** buying veal that is cut in this way, place each piece between two layers of plastic wrap and **BEAT** gently with the end of a rolling pin or a meat mallet until it is thin enough.

MIDWEEK DINNER WITH FAMILY

TIME PLAN

MEATBALLS WITH TOMATO SAUCE AND CRUSTY BREAD
(see page 105)

LIVER WITH ONIONS
(see page 113)

ITALIAN CREAMS
(see page 162)

This is a menu full of strongly flavored, satisfying family favorites. Both the meatballs and crusty bread and the liver with onions go well with a simple green salad. The Italian creams are traditionally served with fresh berries or a fresh fruit purée, for a mouth-tingling finish.

The night before, make up the meatballs, brown them and leave to cool, then store in the fridge, covered with plastic wrap. Prepare the tomato sauce. Trim and remove any membranes from the liver and cut into thin slices (or ask your butcher to do this for you). Wrap well in plastic wrap and store in the fridge. Make the Italian creams and keep well chilled.

PM 6:30 **HEAT** the oven for the meatballs. Arrange in a baking dish and top with the tomato sauce and cheese. Slice the onions for the liver and, if serving, prepare a green salad, but do not dress.

6:45 **PLACE** the meatballs in the oven. Sauté the onions for the liver until they are golden brown. Keep warm on one side.

7:15 **REMOVE** the meatballs from the oven and serve with crusty bread.

7:45 **FINISH** cooking the liver and serve. Dress and serve the salad.

8:15 **REMOVE** the Italian creams from the fridge and serve with berries or a fresh fruit purée, as desired.

PREPARATION NOTES

Good **QUALITY** liver is now widely available in supermarkets, as well as at the butcher. If possible, buy it ready sliced to the thickness you require, with the **MEMBRANES** trimmed off. But do check carefully for any remaining membranes before cooking. They can easily be removed by stripping them off with a **SHARP** knife.

MIDWEEK DINNER WITH FRIENDS

TIME PLAN

WILD MUSHROOM AND SHALLOT TARTS

(see page 54)

MARINATED SWORDFISH

(see page 130)

WARM CANNELLINI BEANS WITH TOMATOES AND HERBS

(see page 145)

"PICK-ME-UP" PUDDING

(see page 169)

This menu is full of traditional, vibrant, rustic flavors. The simply cooked, meaty fish is a good match for the hearty yet fragrant mix of beans, tomatoes, and herbs. Use whatever mushrooms are available for the tarts and do not be afraid to experiment with new varieties.

The day before, make the pastry shells and store in an airtight container. Soak the beans during the day, then cook them in the evening and store in a cool place until ready to use. Prepare the "pick-me-up" pudding and store in the fridge, but leave the dusting of cocoa powder until just before you are ready to serve.

PM
6:00   **COOK** the mushroom filling for the tarts and put to one side. Prepare the marinade for the swordfish.

7:00   **HEAT** the oven for warming the pastry shells.

7:15   **WARM** the pastry shells for about 10 minutes. Leave the swordfish to marinate. Prepare the beans, then set aside, and keep warm. Reheat the mushroom filling and assemble and serve the tarts.

7:45   **COOK** the swordfish and serve with the warm beans.

8:15   **REMOVE** the pudding from the fridge. Dust with the cocoa powder, carry to the table, and serve.

PREPARATION NOTES

Making good **PASTRY** takes a little practice. The important thing to remember is to use a very light touch—the less the pastry is handled, the **BETTER**. Rub the butter into the flour until it just begins to **BLEND** in, then stop; do not be tempted to carry on until every little piece disappears. Treat pastry **GENTLY** and it will always be light and **CRISP**.

DINNER PARTY

TIME PLAN

This special menu is so simple to put together, allowing the cook plenty of time with guests. The creaminess of the gnocchi and gratin is beautifully balanced by the pungent aromas of the fresh herbs and tomatoes. A truly heavenly dessert rounds off the evening perfectly.

SEMOLINA GNOCCHI WITH FRESH TOMATO SAUCE

(see page 93)

LEG OF LAMB WITH HERB CRUST

(see page 114)

POTATO AND HERB GRATIN

(see page 142)

ICE CREAM WITH ESPRESSO AND FRANGELICO

(see page 173)

The night before, prepare the gnocchi dish and the lamb, so that both are ready to go into the oven. Keep them, covered, in the fridge. Scoop ice cream into individual dishes and return to the freezer. Remember that the recipes are written to serve just four people, so you will need to increase the quantities of ingredients if serving larger numbers.

PM

6:30 HEAT the oven.

7:00 PLACE the prepared lamb in the hot oven.

7:40 ADD the prepared gnocchi dish to the oven, alongside the lamb. Prepare the potato gratin.

8:00 REMOVE the gnocchi from the oven and serve. Put the potato gratin into the oven.

8:15 CHECK the lamb and if cooked, remove from the oven, and leave in a warm place to rest 15 minutes.

8:30 SERVE the lamb with the potato gratin.

9:15 REMOVE the ice cream from the freezer, top with the espresso and Frangelico liqueur, and serve immediately.

PREPARATION NOTES

When you buy the leg of LAMB, make sure that you ask the butcher to cut PARTIALLY through the base of the BONE. This will make the roast much easier to carve. Remember, too, that the meat will also slice up more easily if it is allowed to stand, in a WARM place, 10 to 15 minutes after it has finished cooking.

COCKTAIL PARTY

TIME PLAN

A cocktail party is a great way to entertain a large number of people with ease. As well as finger food that can be passed around, try to include several buffet dishes, for eating with a fork, to which guests can help themselves.

CROSTINI WITH GORGONZOLA AND BLACK OLIVE TAPENADE

(see page 42)

DEEP-FRIED RICE BALLS

(see page 57)

CHARBROILED VEGETABLE SALAD

(see page 34)

EGGPLANT WITH TOMATO SAUCE AND CHEESE

(see page 38)

BAKED MUSSELS WITH CRISPY HERB BREADCRUMBS

(see page 37)

The day before, make the crostini and store in an airtight container. Prepare the black olive tapenade and store in the fridge. Prepare the rice balls ready for deep-frying and place, covered, in the fridge. Make up the sauce to accompany them and make up the eggplant, tomato, and cheese dish, ready to go into the oven. Store both in the fridge, covered. Charbroil all the vegetables for the salad and prepare the dressing, then store separately in a cool place. Clean the mussels thoroughly and keep, covered, in the fridge. Note that the recipes serve just four people, so you will need to adjust the quantities of ingredients for larger numbers.

PM
6:30 **HEAT** the oven for the eggplant dish.
7:00 **PLACE** the eggplant dish in the hot oven. Prepare the filling for the mussels. Cook the mussels, discarding any that do not open.
7:20 **REMOVE** the baked eggplant dish from the oven and leave to cool slightly. Spread the topping on the crostini. Assemble and dress the salad. Prepare the stuffed mussels. Heat the oil for the rice balls.
7:30 **COOK** the rice balls until golden and drain. Place the tomato sauce to accompany them in a bowl. Arrange all the food on platters and serve.

PREPARATION NOTES

It is very important to make sure that the **MUSSELS** you use are very fresh. Empty them into a large sink of cold water and **CLEAN** them well, removing any barnacles and the "beard" with a sharp knife. Discard any mussels that remain **OPEN** at this point, as this indicates that the mussel is not fresh.

INDEX